Ethics and Aesthetics of the Instant in the Digital Age

Sergi Castillo Lapeira

Published by edicionsmataro.com, 2024.

ETHICS AND AESTHETICS OF THE INSTANT IN THE DIGITAL AGE

First edition. October 12, 2024.

ISBN: 979-8224819119

Written by Sergi Castillo Lapeira.

Table of Contents

Per a l'Erin i per a en Liam

Per a l'Erin i per a en Liam

0. INTRODUCTION

IN THE CONSTANT FLOW of time, there is a moment that is always with us, but that is often elusive to us: the present. This fleeting moment, this "now" that is always here but that we can never retain, is the focus of this essay on the ethics and aesthetics of the present.

Our experience of the world is inevitably anchored in the present moment, but the nature of this "now" is profoundly paradoxical. How can we conceive of an instant that is both eternal and ephemeral? How can we make ethical decisions or make aesthetic judgments in a moment that seems to disappear as soon as we try to capture it?

This book proposes to explore these issues from multiple perspectives, guided by the following working hypotheses:

1. The perception of the present as an isolated moment is a skill that can be developed and that has significant implications for our ethical and aesthetic judgments.
2. The experience of the pure present is conditioned by cultural and technological factors that influence our ability to perceive and value the moment.
3. The ability to perceive the instant as eternal, while

acknowledging the flow of time, can lead to more reflective ethics and a deeper aesthetic appreciation of reality.

These three general hypotheses make sense within the framework of the following four main objectives that we propose to achieve:

1. Analyse the relationship between the perception of the present and the formation of immediate ethical and aesthetic judgments.
2. To explore how contemplative and artistic practices can modify our experience of the present and, therefore, our ethical decisions and aesthetic appreciations.
3. Examine the impact of digital culture on our ability to perceive and value the isolated present.
4. To analyse the different ontological conceptions of the instant and to assess how they affect our understanding and experience of the ethics and aesthetics of the present.

At the end of this work, we want to demonstrate, as far as our limitations allow us, the following theses:

1. The development of the ability to perceive the present as an isolated instant can lead to more conscious ethical judgments and a deeper aesthetic appreciation of immediate reality.
2. The ethics and aesthetics of the present are intrinsically linked and influence each other in our

immediate experience of the world.

3. Contemporary culture, especially in the digital age, presents challenges that call into question the possibility of achieving the perception of a "pure present", but also offers new opportunities for the ethical and aesthetic experience of the moment.

4. Although the instant can be ontologically questioned in the face of the unstoppable temporal flow, its phenomenological reality is undeniable and fundamental to our ethical and aesthetic experience of the world.

We will begin by examining how we perceive the present, questioning whether this perception is innate or learned. We will delve into the ontology of the instant, challenging its existence in the face of the unstoppable avalanche of the flow of time. And we will explore the paradox of the eternal instant, looking for strategies to maintain awareness of the present in a world of continuous change.

As we move forward, we will find out how this understanding of the present influences our ethical decisions and our aesthetic appreciations. How does the immediacy of the moment affect our ability to make moral judgments? How does it influence our perception of beauty? And how do these ethical and aesthetic aspects interact in our experience of the present?

In an era dominated by digital immediacy and constant acceleration, these issues take on special relevance. Our ability to perceive and value the present can have profound implications for our personal and collective ethics, as well as for the aesthetic appreciation of the world around us.

This work does not intend and cannot offer definitive answers, but rather to open a space for reflection on how we experience, value and act in this eternal "now". Through an interdisciplinary exploration spanning philosophy, anthropology, physics, mathematics, and art, we will seek to deepen our understanding of the ethics and aesthetics of the present, hoping to enrich the experience of that "instant" that is always with us.

1. THE PERCEPTION OF THE PRESENT: AN ANTHROPOLOGICAL PERSPECTIVE

THE PERCEPTION OF THE present, despite being an apparently universal and immediate experience, is actually a complex phenomenon that is deeply influenced by cultural, social and historical factors. Anthropology, with its holistic and comparative view, offers us a unique perspective to understand how human beings, in different societies and times, experience and conceptualize "the now".

From an anthropological perspective, the perception of the present is not a simple biological function, but a cultural construction that varies significantly between societies. This variation manifests itself in the everyday practices, rituals, social structures, belief systems, and linguistic patterns of different cultures.

For example, while in many modern Western societies the present is conceived as a fleeting point between the past and the future, other cultures have more expansive or cyclical conceptions of time. Some indigenous societies, for example, may perceive the present as a broader temporal space that includes elements of the recent past and the immediate future.

Anthropology also shows us how the perception of the present is intimately linked to the ways of life and livelihoods of a society. In traditional farming communities, for example, the perception of the present can be much more linked to natural and seasonal cycles than in industrialised urban societies, where time is measured in a more abstract and fragmented way.

In addition, anthropological study reveals how power structures and social hierarchies influence who has the "right" to define and control the present. In many societies, control over the definition and use of the present tense is an important form of social and political power.

Linguistic anthropology, on the other hand, has shown how different languages encode and express time and the present in different ways, thus influencing how speakers perceive and experience "the now". Some languages, for example, do not have verb tenses in the Western sense, suggesting a radically different experience of time and present.

In the era of globalization and digitalization, anthropology faces new challenges and opportunities in the study of the perception of the present. Global interconnectedness and digital technologies are creating new ways of experiencing "the now", including experiences of simultaneity and immediacy that transcend traditional geographical boundaries.

Understanding the perception of the present from an anthropological perspective has profound implications for ethics and aesthetics. Ethical decisions and aesthetic appreciations are deeply rooted in how we experience the present moment. A culture that values an expansive and contemplative present may have a very different approach to ethical and aesthetic issues compared to one that experiences the present as fleeting and fragmented.

In the following subchapters, we will explore in detail various aspects of the perception of the present from an anthropological perspective. We will examine how this perception is learned, how it relates to the subjective interpretation of reality, and what are the possibilities and limitations of conceiving the present as an isolated instant. This exploration will not only help us better understand the diversity of human experience, but will also provide us with new perspectives to reflect on our own perception of the present and its ethical and aesthetic implications.

1.1. Learning perception

PERCEPTION, ALTHOUGH it seems an innate and immediate capacity, is to a large extent a process learned and shaped by experience. This is especially true when we talk about the perception of time and, more specifically, the present.

From birth, humans begin to develop the ability to perceive and interpret the world around them. This perceptual learning process is not limited only to sight, hearing or touch, but also includes our perception of time and the present.

Studies in developmental psychology have shown that children are not born with a fully formed perception of time. In the first months of life, babies live in a continuous present, without a clear distinction between past, present and future. It is through experience and interaction with their environment that they begin to develop a sense of time and, by extension, of the present.[1]

The process of learning to perceive the present is intimately linked to cognitive development and language acquisition. As children learn to speak and use verb tenses, they begin to conceptualize tense in more sophisticated ways. The use of words such as "now", "before" and "after" marks a turning point in his understanding of the present as a moment different from the past and the future.

Culture plays a crucial role in this learning process. The parenting practices, social rituals and everyday activities of a society shape the way children learn to perceive and value the present. For example, in Japanese culture, the concept of "hand" (◇?) It teaches children to value intervals or pauses between events as significant parts of the present. This can influence how they perceive silence in a conversation or empty space in a visual composition.[2]

In contrast, in many Western societies, children can learn to perceive the present as a rapid succession of events. Carefully planned extracurricular activities, for example, can teach children to perceive the present as highly structured segments of time.

In some Amazonian indigenous communities, children learn to perceive the present in relation to natural cycles. For example, they can learn to recognize the "present of the rainy season" or the "present of the flowering of a certain plant", developing a perception of time more linked to the natural environment.

Formal education also has a significant impact on how we learn to perceive the present. The structure of school days, with rigid schedules and timed activities, instills a certain way of perceiving and valuing the present time. For example, in Montessori schools, children work in uninterrupted blocks of time of up to three hours, encouraging a more expansive and task-focused perception of the present. In contrast, the traditional education system with 50-60 minute classes can promote a more fragmented and short-term goal-oriented perception of the present.

Art or music classes can teach students to perceive the present differently. For example, in a life drawing class, students learn to observe and capture the immediate present, developing a keener perception of the visual "now".

It is important to note that learning to perceive the present is not limited to childhood. Throughout life, our experiences continue to shape how we perceive and experience "the now." Practices such as meditation or mindfulness, for example, can be seen as ways to train our perception of the present, teaching us to focus our attention on the present moment.

In the digital age, we are learning new ways of perceiving the present. The immediacy of information and constant connectivity are reshaping our experience of the "now," creating an expanded sense of present that includes distant events and multiple simultaneous streams of information. The use of social networks such as "X" or TikTok can teach us to perceive the present as a rapid succession of brief and intense moments. Multiplayer online games teach players to perceive multiple simultaneous "presents": the present of the game, the present of communication with other players, and the present of the physical world around them. On the other hand, mindfulness apps such as Headspace or Calm are teaching millions of users to perceive the present in a more conscious and detailed way.

This process of learning perception has significant implications for ethics and aesthetics. The way we learn to perceive the present directly influences how we make ethical decisions and how we aesthetically appreciate the world around us. For example, a more contemplative perception of the present can lead to more thoughtful ethical judgments and a deeper aesthetic appreciation of the immediate environment.

Understanding that the perception of the present is a learned skill opens up the possibility of rethinking and potentially reshaping our experience of "the now". This has not only personal implications, but also collective ones, as the way a society perceives and values the present has a profound impact on its social structures, value systems and cultural expressions.

Finally, it is important to recognise that different professions and practices can teach us to perceive the present in very different ways. A stock trader can learn to perceive the present in intervals of seconds or milliseconds, where every moment can mean significant gains or losses. A Buddhist monk practicing Vipassana meditation He can learn to perceive the present as a continuous flow of momentary bodily sensations. A street photographer can develop the ability to perceive and capture "decisive moments" in the constant flow of the urban present. An improvising jazz musician can learn to perceive the present as a space of creative possibilities in constant evolution.

These diverse examples illustrate how learning to perceive the present is a complex and multifaceted process, influenced by a wide range of cultural, educational and experiential factors. Understanding this diversity allows us to appreciate the richness of human experiences of the "now" and opens up new possibilities for the ethical and aesthetic exploration of the present.

1.2. Reality and its subjective interpretation

THE PERCEPTION OF THE present not only implies how we experience time, but also how we interpret the reality that surrounds us at each moment. From an anthropological perspective, "reality" is not an objective and uniform entity, but is profoundly influenced by the subjective interpretation of each individual and each culture.

Phenomenology, a branch of philosophy that has significantly influenced anthropology, argues that our experience of the world is always mediated by our consciousness. In other words, we do not experience a "naked" reality, but a reality interpreted through our cultural perceptions, beliefs, and expectations.

This subjective interpretation of reality manifests itself in several ways:

1. Cultural filters: Each culture provides its members with a set of "lenses" through which they interpret the world. For example, in some Amazonian cultures, certain sounds of the jungle may be interpreted as messages from the spirits, while in a Western urban culture, the same sounds might simply be ignored or interpreted as ambient noise.

2. Language: The language we speak influences how we perceive and categorize reality. The anthropologist and linguist Benjamin Lee Whorf proposed that linguistic structures can influence cognition and

perception, in the known *Sapir-Whorf hypothesis* or *Linguistic determinism*. This theory suggests that the language we speak has a decisive influence on the way we perceive and think about the world.[3] In the same line of work, Stephen C. Levinson and others have studied the relationship between language and spatial orientation in Australian Aboriginal groups. For example, some languages in these areas use cardinal directions (north, south, east, west) instead of egocentric terms such as "right" or "left", which can influence how speakers perceive and navigate space.[4]

3. Previous experiences: Our past experiences shape how we interpret the present. A trained anthropologist can "see" cultural patterns in a scene that would otherwise go unnoticed.

4. Altered states of consciousness: Many cultures use techniques to alter consciousness (such as meditation, rituals, or the use of psychoactive substances) that can radically change the perception of present reality.

5. Social context: Our interpretation of reality is influenced by our social role and the expectations of others. For example, how a shaman interprets reality during a ritual can be very different from how he or she does it in everyday life.

6. Technology: The tools and technologies we use also shape our perception of reality. The widespread use of smartphones, for example, has changed how many people perceive and interact with their immediate environment.

The subjectivity of the interpretation of reality has profound implications for ethics and aesthetics:

Ethics: If reality is subjective, how can we establish universal ethical norms? Anthropology shows us that ethical judgments are often deeply rooted in specific cultural interpretations of reality.

Aesthetics: Beauty, as a subjective experience, is intrinsically linked to how we interpret reality. What is considered beautiful or aesthetically pleasing can vary greatly between cultures and individuals.

However, it is important to note that recognizing the subjectivity of the interpretation of reality does not imply absolute relativism. Contemporary anthropology recognizes that, although interpretations of reality are diverse, there are certain human universals and points of convergence between cultures. From Kant to Marta Nussbaum, John Rawls, Peter Singer or Steven Pinker, there is a long philosophical tradition that has defended its existence.

In addition, the human capacity for reflexivity – that is, the ability to reflect on our own perceptions and interpretations – allows us to question and potentially transcend our own cultural biases.

In the context of the perception of the present, this subjectivity means that the "now" we experience is not simply an objective moment in time, but a complex construction influenced by multiple cultural and individual factors. Understanding this subjectivity allows us to appreciate the richness and diversity of the human experience of the present, while inviting us to reflect critically on our own interpretations of reality.

1.3. The present as an isolated instant: possibilities and limitations

THE CONCEPTION OF THE present as an isolated instant, completely separated from the past and the future, offers a particular perspective on the nature of human experience. This idea has been explored by various thinkers throughout history. Philosophers such as Henri Bergson, which developed the concept of "pure duration", an experience of time without the influence of the past or the future, Martin Heidegger, with its concept of "Dasein" and the emphasis on the immediate experience of being, and Jean-Paul Sartre, which explored the idea of radical freedom in the present moment, are a good example.

In the artistic field, there is the example of John Cage, composer who experimented with random music and silence, emphasizing the immediate experience of sound, Marina Abramović, a performative artist known for her works that explore the presence and awareness of the moment, or Yves Klein, with his monochromatic paintings that seek to capture the essence of a single color in an instant.

Also from spirituality we can find different examples of people who have cultivated the experience of the eternal instant, such as Thich Nhat Hanh, Vietnamese Zen master who has taught extensively on the practice of mindfulness in the present moment, Eckhart Tolle, a spiritual author who has popularized the idea of living in the "now" through his books and teachings, or Jiddu Krishnamurti, which emphasized the importance of direct and immediate observation of reality.

These thinkers, artists and practitioners, among many others, each from their own perspective and discipline, have contributed to the exploration and development of the idea of the present as an isolated instant, an idea that, however, presents both transformative possibilities and significant limitations.

One of the main possibilities of this perspective is the intensification of sensory experience. For example, in mindfulness practice, participants often report a keener perception of details in their environment: the distant sound of a bird, the texture of a leaf, or shades of color in a landscape that would normally go unnoticed.

The conception of the present as an isolated fact can also foster a sense of freedom and spontaneity. In the context of psychological therapy, techniques such as Acceptance and Commitment Therapy (ACT) use this approach to help patients break free from negative thought patterns rooted in the past, allowing them to make freer and more authentic decisions in the present.

In the artistic field, the idea of the isolated present has inspired unique forms of expression. A clear example is "action painting" by Jackson Pollock, where the artist immerses himself completely in the act of painting, creating works that are the result of spontaneous and unrepeatable improvisation.

However, this perspective also has significant limitations. In the field of cultural appreciation, for example, trying to experience the Sagrada Família of Barcelona as a mere visual instant, without considering its history and context, could result in a significantly impoverished experience.

In interpersonal relationships, the importance of the temporal context becomes evident. Let's imagine a couple celebrating their birthday: much of the meaning and emotion of this moment comes precisely from the shared history and future expectations, elements that are lost if each moment is conceived as completely isolated.

Ethically, the conception of the present as an isolated moment presents important challenges. For example, in the context of climate change, a perspective focused solely on the present could justify actions that, while comfortable or beneficial in the short term, have catastrophic consequences in the long term.

Faced with these possibilities and limitations, many have come to the conclusion that the most beneficial thing is to seek a balance. In photography, for example, a photographer can fully immerse themselves in the moment to capture a unique image, but they also consider how that image will be integrated into a larger series or narrative.

In medical practice, healthcare professionals must balance the need to be fully present and attentive to each patient, while maintaining a broader perspective that includes medical history and long-term treatment considerations.

By way of conclusion, we can affirm that the exploration of the present as an isolated instant offers valuable perspectives on the nature of human perception and consciousness. The poet William Blake captured this idea in his famous verse "To see a world in a grain of sand"[5], suggesting the possibility of perceiving infinity in an instant. However, as we have seen, this perspective has its limitations.

Ultimately, the ability to fully immerse oneself in the present, combined with the ability to connect that present with the larger context of our lives, can lead to a richer and more nuanced experience of existence. This balanced approach allows us to take advantage of the transformative possibilities of the "now" without losing sight of the complexity and interconnection of the temporal flow in which we are immersed.

1.4 The technological revolution of the present: A journey into the future of temporal perception

LET'S IMAGINE OURSELVES in the not-too-distant future. Maria, a 27-year-old woman, wakes up in a world where technology has completely redefined our experience of time and the present.

Her day begins as usual, but today she decides to experiment with her temporal perception. With a simple thought, it activates its non-invasive brain-computer interface. Suddenly, his sense of the present expands. Every second seems to last forever, allowing you to appreciate every detail of your surroundings with amazing clarity. This technology, an evolutionary step beyond primitive smartphones and virtual reality glasses, allows you to modulate your temporary experience without the need for invasive surgery.

As she prepares to leave, Maria reflects on how quantum computing has transformed her reality. Virtual reality environments generated by quantum computers are now indistinguishable from the physical world. Last night, he spent what seemed like hours exploring a perfect recreation of ancient Rome, though his biological clock, genetically modified to optimize his circadian rhythm, tells him it was only minutes in "real-time."

Once on the street, Maria finds herself immersed in a world augmented by advanced holograms. Advertisements, information, and even virtual people populate your visual field, creating an extra layer of "present" that overlays physical reality. Thanks to predictive AI, receives notifications of events that have not yet happened, blurring the line between the present and the immediate future.

On his way to work, he passes a cryogenics clinic. He wonders, like so many others, if he will one day dare to "pause" his life temporarily, thus challenging his linear understanding of time. The idea of waking up decades or centuries in the future produces a mixture of fascination and vertigo.

Once in the office, he participates in a meeting using "synthetic reality" technology". It is located in a virtual space indistinguishable from reality, where the laws of time can be altered at will. The meeting, which subjectively lasts for hours, occupies only minutes in the outside world.

After work, Maria decides to try a new neurodrug specifically designed to alter temporal perception. The experience is intense: the present stretches like an elastic band, allowing him to explore each moment with a depth previously unimaginable. He wonders if this resembles the experience of the "eternal instant" that the mystics of the past spoke of.

Before going to bed, he activates his sleep control device. Tonight, he will experience a dreamlike adventure that will subjectively last for weeks, although he will only sleep for a few hours. Dream-modifying technology has opened up a whole new realm of temporal experience, challenging conventional notions of duration and continuity.

As she falls asleep, Maria reflects on how these technologies have transformed not only her perception of time, but also her understanding of reality itself. The distinction between past, present and future seems increasingly arbitrary. The "present" is no longer a fixed point in a timeline, but a fluid and malleable space.

These new technologies have opened up fascinating possibilities, but they have also raised unsettling questions. How does this manipulation of time affect our identity and our relationships? What are the ethical implications of being able to "edit" our temporal experience? And perhaps most importantly, in a world where time is so fluid, what defines our humanity?

Maria's story is just a taste of what the future of temporal perception could be. From quantum computing to the genetic manipulation of the circadian rhythm, through synthetic reality and neuropharmaceuticals, each technological advance opens up new dimensions in our experience of the present.

But with these new capabilities also come new responsibilities. Society faces the challenge of ethically navigating this new temporal landscape. How can we harness these technologies to enrich our lives without losing connection to our essential humanity? How can we ensure that access to these augmented temporary experiences does not create new forms of inequality?

Ultimately, these emerging technologies are not only redefining how we perceive time, but they are challenging our fundamental understanding of what it means to exist in the present. In this new world, the ability to consciously navigate between different "layers" of time and reality could become one of the most decisive skills for a full and meaningful life.

As we look to the future, one thing seems obvious: our relationship with time is about to change in ways we can't even fully imagine. The challenge and opportunity before us is to learn to live with this new rhythm of time, maintaining our humanity while exploring the vast possibilities that open up before us.

2. ONTOLOGY OF THE INSTANT: REALITY OR ILLUSION IN THE FLOW OF TIME?

WHEN WE TRY TO CAPTURE the present, we are faced with a paradox: the instant seems to be both omnipresent and unattainable. This fleeting "now", this hinge between the past and the future, is the core of what we call the ontology of the instant.

But what exactly do we mean by "ontology of the instant"? Ontology is concerned with the fundamental nature of being, its essence and existence. Applied to the instant, it leads us to ask: does the instant really exist as an independent entity? Or is it simply a mental construct, an illusion created by our way of perceiving the continuous flow of time?

This question places us at the heart of a dichotomy: reality versus fiction. If the instant is real, we should be able to isolate it, define it, perhaps even measure it. But how can we do this if, by definition, the instant has no duration? And if it is a fiction, how do we explain our lived experience of "the now", this intense and immediate sensation of the present?

The distinction between fact and fiction in this context is not merely academic. It greatly affects how we understand our existence over time. If the instant is real, perhaps we live in a granular universe, made up of discrete moments. If it is an illusion, perhaps our perception of time is radically different from its true nature.

This tension between reality and fiction in the ontology of the instant manifests itself on multiple levels. In our everyday experience, we feel the weight of the "now" as something undeniably real. But when we try to analyze it, it dissolves between our conceptual fingers. In classical physics, the instant plays a crucial role in our equations, but relativity and quantum mechanics question its absolute nature.

Einstein's theory of special relativity proved that the concept of a universal or absolute instant is invalid. What is simultaneous (and therefore "in an instant") for one observer may not be so for another in relative motion.

A relevant quote on this issue is from Albert Einstein himself:

"The simultaneity of two successive events (or, in general, the temporal order of two events in space) depends on the observer's frame of reference."[6]

For its part, quantum mechanics It introduces uncertainty in the precise measurement of time at very small scales, making the concept of a well-defined "instant" problematic at the subatomic level.

A quote that illustrates this idea is from Werner Heisenberg:

"In the strong formulation of the causal principle, 'If we know the present exactly, we can calculate the future', it is not the conclusion that is incorrect, but the premise."[7]

The physicist and philosopher Carlo Rovelli offers an interesting perspective on how modern physics treats the instant:

"The time of physics does not flow, it does not happen. There is no universal present that 'advances'. Events are not ordered into past, present and future; they are only ordered in their mutual relations." [8]

These insights from modern physics suggest that while the instant is a useful concept in our everyday experience, its nature at a fundamental level is more complex and far less "absolute" than intuition tells us.

2.1. Philosophical conceptualizations of the instant.

THE INSTANT, THAT FLEETING point between the past and the future, has intrigued philosophers for millennia. Its seemingly paradoxical nature – being both ubiquitous and intangible – has spawned a rich tradition of philosophical thought. We analyze some of the most influential conceptualizations of the moment throughout the history of philosophy.

2.1.1. Classical and Medieval Perspectives

IN GREEK ANTIQUITY, the notion of the instant was the subject of intense philosophical reflection, giving rise to various conceptions that have influenced Western thought to this day.

Heraclitus (c. 535-475 BCE) conceived of time as a constant flow, an idea captured in his famous phrase "You cannot enter the same river twice". For Heraclitus, the instant was not a fixed point in time, but a moment of transition in the constant evolution of the world. This vision emphasizes the dynamic and changing nature of reality, where every moment is unique and unrepeatable. The Heraclitian conception suggests that the instant, despite being momentary, is charged with the totality of the temporal flow.

In marked opposition, Parmenides (c. 515-450 BCE) proposed a view of reality as static and eternal. He argued that change is impossible and that the true nature of being is immutable. This perspective radically questions the very notion of the instant as a fleeting moment. In the world of Parmenides, we could say that there is only one eternal "now", immune to the passage of time. This idea, although it seems counterintuitive, has had a profound influence on later philosophy, especially on the conceptions of eternity and the immutable.

Zeno of Elea (c. 490-430 BC), a follower of Parmenides, formulated a series of paradoxes that question the logical coherence of movement and, by extension, of time and instant. The paradox of the arrow, for example, argues that at any indivisible instant, an arrow in flight is motionless. If time is made up of instants, how can there be movement? These paradoxes are not mere logical puzzles, but point to fundamental problems in our understanding of the continuity and divisibility of time.[9]

Plato (428/427-348/347 BC), in his dialogue "Timaeus" [10], introduced the idea of time as a "moving image of eternity". This conception establishes a crucial distinction between the temporal world, characterized by change and the succession of instants, and the eternal world of Forms. For Plato, the instants of time are like projected shadows of immutable eternity. This vision raises relevant questions about the relationship between the temporal instant and eternal reality, a theme that has resonated throughout the history of philosophy.

Aristotle (384-322 BC) offered a more systematic analysis of time in his "Physics"[11]. He defined time as "the measure of movement according to the before and after". "If nothing changes, time does not exist." For Aristotle, the instant (το νῦν, "to nun", the now) is what divides the past from the future and gives continuity to time. However, he argued that the instant is not a part of time, but a limit, comparable to a point on a line. This conception of the instant as a limit or hinge between past and future has had a lasting influence on the philosophy of time.

In late antiquity, St. Augustine (354-430 AD) offered a profound and influential reflection on the nature of time and the instant in Book XI of his "Confessions"[12]. He conceived of the present as an "instant without duration" that constantly passes from the future to the past. This paradoxical idea of an instant that exists but has no temporal extension has had a lasting influence on Western thought. Augustine writes:

"If any time can be conceived that cannot be divided into minimal parts of instants, only this can be called present. And this time flies so quickly from the future to the past, that it has no duration. Because if it did, it would be divided into past and future."[13]

Augustine also explored the psychological nature of time, suggesting that the past and future exist only in the mind, while the present is the only temporal reality. This psychological perspective of time opens up new ways of understanding the instant not only as an objective phenomenon, but as a subjective experience.[14]

A century later Boethius (c. 480-524) offered new and sophisticated reflections on the instant. In "The Consolation of Philosophy", contrasted divine eternity with human temporality. He conceived of the instant as the point of contact between these two realms, suggesting that the human experience of the instant is a limited participation in divine eternity.[15]

In medieval times, Avicenna (980-1037), a Persian philosopher and physician, argued that the instant is not a part of time, but its limit, similar to how a point is the limit of a line. This conception, influenced by Aristotle, had a significant impact on later scholastic thought. Avicenna explored how the instant, although it has no duration, can be the moment of change, an idea that would later be developed by other medieval thinkers, such as Thomas Aquinas or William of Ockham.

Moses Maimonides (1138-1204), in his work "Guide to the Perplexed"[16], explored the relationship between the instant, movement and creation. He argued that time is necessarily linked to movement and, therefore, to creation. This perspective raises questions about the nature of time before the creation of the world and about the relationship between the instant and divine eternity. At the same time, he defends an atomistic or discrete vision of time: "Time is composed of atoms, that is, of many parts that cannot be subdivided any further, due to their short duration."[17]

Thomas Aquinas (1225-1274) developed the idea of the instant as the "indivisible of time" and explored its relationship to substantial change and divine eternity. For Aquino, the instant, although it has no duration, can be the moment of change. He argued that at the instant of substantial change, the old form ceases to exist and the new one begins to exist simultaneously. This conception tries to reconcile the continuity of time with the possibility of discrete changes.

William of Ockham (c. 1287-1347) proposed a nominalist view of time and instant, arguing that they have no real existence outside the mind, but are mental constructions based on movement and change. This perspective anticipates to some extent modern conceptions that see time as a cognitive structure rather than as an objective reality.

These medieval reflections established a basic bridge between ancient and modern conceptions of the instant, introducing new subtleties in the understanding of the relationship between time, change, eternity and human experience. They prepared the ground for the conceptual revolutions that would come with the arrival of modernity.

2.1.2. Modern and Contemporary Visions

WITH THE ADVENT OF modernity, the conceptualizations of the instant took new directions, influenced by advances in science and mathematics, as well as by new philosophical perspectives.

René Descartes (1596-1650) introduced a notion of temporal discontinuity that had profound implications for the understanding of the instant. In his metaphysics, Descartes suggested that every moment of existence requires a continuous "recreation" by God. This idea implies that existence in one instant does not necessarily guarantee existence in the next. Descartes writes in his "Metaphysical Meditations":

"It is, indeed, a very clear and obvious thing to all who consider attentively the nature of time, that a substance, in order to exist at every moment that lasts, needs the same force and action that would be necessary to produce and create it again if it did not exist."[18]

This perspective opens up the possibility of conceiving the instant as a discrete and independent entity, rather than as part of an uninterrupted temporal continuum.

Nicolas Malebranche (1638-1715) further developed this idea with his concept of "continuous creation". According to Malebranche, God not only creates the world initially, but recreates it at every moment. This occasionalist view leads to a conception of the instant as fundamentally discontinuous and dependent on constant divine action. Malebranche writes:

"God not only creates all things at the beginning of his existence: he produces and preserves them without ceasing." [19]

This perspective raises questions about the nature of causality and temporal continuity, suggesting that each instant could be ontologically independent of the others.

Immanuel Kant (1724-1804) provoked a revolution in the philosophical understanding of time and the instant. In his "Critique of Pure Reason"", Kant proposed that time, and therefore the instant, is not a property of things in themselves, but an a priori form of our sensible intuition. According to Kant, time is a structure that the mind imposes on experience, rather than an objective characteristic of reality. Kant writes:

"Time is nothing more than the form of the inner sense, that is, of the intuition of ourselves and of our inner state."[20]

This transcendental perspective argues that our experience of the instant is fundamentally shaped by the structures of our cognition, opening up new ways to understand the relationship between subjectivity and temporality.

Georg Wilhelm Friedrich Hegel (1770 - 1831), one of the most influential philosophers of the nineteenth century, offers a unique vision of the instant within his philosophical system. In his work, Hegel understands the instant not as an isolated or static moment, but as an integral part of the dialectical process of the development of the Spirit (*Geist*).

For Hegel, reality develops through a constant movement of theses, antitheses, and syntheses. This dialectical process is temporal and historical, and each instant represents a transition point in this flow. The instant is, therefore, a synthesis of past moments and an anticipation of futures. It is not a separate fragment of time, but an expression of the continuous evolution of the absolute idea. Hegel writes:

"What I indicate is an Now that has already ceased to be at the moment I indicate it. The Now that is has already ceased to be; the Now that was is no more; it is an Now that has been. But what has been is not in reality; what is, however, is another Now. [...] The Now is, therefore, that being that at the same time is not; it is the non-being that is and the being that is not." [21]

This passage is a clear example of Hegel's dialectical thought, where the instant (the Now) is revealed as a contradiction between being and non-being. According to Hegel, the instant or Now is not a fixed reality, but a moment in a constant process of change. When we try to capture the Now as the present, it has already ceased to be so and has become the past. Thus, the Now is revealed as a contradiction: to be in a moment, but, at the same time, no longer to be. This contradiction between being and non-being reflects the dialectical nature of time, which develops through what Hegel calls "becoming", a continuous process in which every moment of reality is immediately transformed into another.

For Hegel, the present cannot be understood as something stable, but as the synthesis of what has been and what is to come. Each instant denies the previous moment, but this negation is not a total destruction: it is a Overcoming (in German, *Aufhebung*) that preserves what has happened, but transforming it. Thus, the Now is a point of transition between the past and the future, never a definitive or complete reality.

This concept illustrates his conception of reality as a process: nothing is permanent, but everything is in constant movement and change. This makes immediate knowledge of reality (such as the attempt to trap the Now) deceptive, because reality itself is always in motion, denying and surpassing itself at every moment.

Henri Bergson (1859-1941) offered a radical critique of mathematical and scientific conceptions of time, introducing the concept of "duration" (duration). For Bergson, real time is a continuous and indivisible experience, in contrast to the mathematical conception of discrete instants. In his work "Essay on the Immediate Data of Consciousness", Bergson argues:

"Pure duration is the form that the succession of our states of consciousness takes when our ego allows itself to live, when it refrains from establishing a separation between the present state and the previous states."[22]

This view of duration as a continuous flow questions the notion of the instant as a discrete point in time, suggesting instead a constant interpenetration of past, present, and future in our lived experience.

Martin Heidegger (1889-1976) provided a unique existential perspective on the instant with his concept of "Augenblick" (moment of vision). For Heidegger, Augenblick is not simply a point in chronological time, but a moment of revelation and authentic decision. In his work "Being and Time", Heidegger writes:

"The phenomenon of the instant cannot be clarified from now on. The now is a temporal phenomenon that belongs to time as intratemporality: the now 'in which' something arises, happens or is present. In the instant there is nothing that can arise, but, as its own resolution, the ecstatic presentation opens up the situation and keeps it open."[23]

This conception of the instant as a moment of deep existential meaning offers a radically different perspective from the more mathematical or physical visions of time. For Heidegger, Augenblick is not simply a point in a temporal sequence, but a moment of authentic revelation and existential decision. The concept is based on the distinction between the "now" (Jetzt), which belongs to the everyday and inauthentic understanding of time, and the Augenblick, which represents a more authentic and profound way of experiencing temporality. Augenblick is not a moment in which something "happens", but a moment of existential openness where Dasein (the being, the human being in his existence) is confronted with its most proper possibilities.

2.1.3. Crisis of classical logical conceptions of the instant

IN CONTEMPORARY THOUGHT, traditional conceptions of the instant have come under even deeper scrutiny, influenced by advances in physics, mathematics and philosophy.

Albert Einstein's theory of relativity (1879-1955) radically transformed our understanding of time and, by extension, of the instant. We have seen how special relativity introduced the notion of relative simultaneity, suggesting that there is no universal "now".

Quantum mechanics has brought new challenges to the conception of the instant. The uncertainty principle of Werner Heisenberg (1901-1976) suggests that there are fundamental limits to the precision with which we can simultaneously measure certain pairs of physical properties, such as the position and momentum of a particle. This raises relevant questions about the nature of the instant at subatomic scales. Niels Bohr (1885-1962) reflected on these implications:

"In the great drama of existence, we are both actors and spectators."[24]

This idea argues for a complex interrelationship between the observer and the observed instant, blurring the lines between subjectivity and objectivity in our understanding of time. The quote reflects Bohr's view of the nature of reality and the role of the observer in quantum physics. It indicates that we are not simply passive observers of the universe, but also actively participate in its creation and interpretation.

In philosophy, new logical approaches have offered alternative perspectives for conceptualizing the instant:

Fuzzy logic, developed by Lotfi Zadeh (1921-2017), allows truth degrees between 0 and 1. Applied instantly, it could allow us to conceive of it as partially present or with diffuse limits, better reflecting our subjective experience of "the now". Zadeh thus expresses what is known as the "Principle of incompatibility":

"As the complexity of a system increases, our ability to make accurate and meaningful claims about its behavior decreases to a threshold beyond which accuracy and relevance become almost mutually exclusive."[25]

The present moment, although it seems simple, is actually a highly complex system that involves multiple neurological, sensory and cognitive processes. Following Zadeh's principle, as we try to describe this instant more precisely, we lose some of its relevance or experiential significance. Thus, determined by this principle, our perception of the instant becomes such a complex task that it becomes impossible, according to our limited cognitive capacities, to obtain precise data on this temporal phenomenon that configures what we call "the now" or "the present".

In this sense, The philosopher Henri Bergson Claims:

"Our perception of the present is already memory... The pure present, that indivisible instant that separates the past from the future, would exist only as an ideal abstraction."[26]

This quote from Bergson illustrates how, in trying to define or perceive the instant precisely, we encounter the limitations described by Zadeh's principle of incompatibility, which are concretized in different types of contradictions:

in. Contradictions between immediacy and memory: Bergson suggests that the moment we perceive the "present", it has already become the past. Like that, there is a tension between our immediate experience and the process of recording that experience.

b. Contradictions between continuity and divisibility: The present is perceived as a continuous flow, but we try to understand it by dividing it into discrete instants.

c. Contradictions between lived experience and conceptualization: There is a tension between how we experience the present in an experiential way and how we try to define or understand it conceptually.

d. Contradictions between reality and abstraction: Bergson suggests that the "pure present" is an ideal abstraction, indicating a tension between our actual experience of time and our attempts to isolate a perfect "instant."

e. Contradictions between perception and cognition: The tension between immediate perception and the cognitive process that tries to capture and understand that perception.

In conclusion, the Principle of Incompatibility helps us understand why the experience of the present moment, despite being fundamental to our consciousness, is so difficult to define and describe accurately without losing its essence and meaning. This perspective forces us to make a more holistic and less rigid appreciation of our temporal experience.

A possible answer is found in paraconsistent logic, developed by philosophers such as Newton da Costa (1929-), which allows the existence of contradictions without trivializing the logical system. This could allow conceptions of the instant that are apparently contradictory, such as being and not being simultaneously. Graham Priest, a contemporary proponent of this theory, argues:

"There are truths that are also false. And there are falsehoods that are also truths."[27]

The "dialectic" by Priest allows us to consider the instant as something that is and is not simultaneously, thus transcending the limitations of binary logic. Interestingly, in quantum physics, phenomena such as the superposition of states (where a particle can be in multiple states simultaneously) find an interesting parallelism with this view of the instant, since in both cases the principle of non-contradiction is violated.

The temporal logic, developed by Arthur Prior (1914-1969), incorporates temporary operators directly into logic. This allows for a more sophisticated treatment of concepts such as "always", "sometimes" and "now", offering new tools for analysing the instant in relation to other temporal structures.

The basic operators of Prior's temporal logic are:

1. P: "It was the case that" (past)
2. F: "It will be the case that" (future)
3. H: "It's always been the case that" (past)
4. G: "It will always be the case that" (future)

In addition, additional operators can be defined as:

1. N: "Now is the case that" (present)

Using these operators, we can express complex propositions about time and the present moment. For example:

- N(p): "p is true now"
- F(p): "p will be true at some point in the future"
- G(p): "p will always be true in the future"

- P(p): "p was true at some point in the past"
- H(p): "p has always been true in the past"

This formalization allows us to analyze the present moment in relation to other temporal structures in a more precise way. For example:

1. Continuity of the present: $N(p) \rightarrow FP(p)$ (If p is true now, in the future it will be true that p was true in the past)

2. Transience of the instant: $N(p) \rightarrow F(P(p) \wedge \neg N(p))$ (If p is true now, in the future it will be true that p was true in the past but is no longer true now)

3. Instant as a bridge between past and future: $G(P(p) \rightarrow p) \wedge H(F(p) \rightarrow p) \rightarrow p$ (If always in the future it will be true that if p was true in the past, p is true, and always in the past it was true that if p will be true in the future, p is true, then p is true now)[28]

Prior's temporal logic also makes it possible to address complex philosophical questions about the nature of time and instant:

- Determinism vs. Indeterminism: Temporal logic can shape different conceptions of the future, allowing the formal analysis of questions about determinism.

- Eternism vs. Presentism: We can use temporal logic to formalize and compare different metaphysical theories about the existence of the past and the future.

- Branching Time: Prior developed "branched time" models that allow alternative futures to be represented, offering a powerful tool for analyzing contingency and freedom.

- A-Series vs. B-Series: Prior's temporal logic is particularly suitable for modeling McTaggart's A-Series perspective (past-present-future), but it can also be adapted to represent B-Series relationships (before -after -simultaneous to).

A specific example of an application is the analysis of the mobile "now":

$$N(p) \wedge F(P(p) \wedge N(q))$$

This formula expresses that p is true now, and at some point in the future it will be true that p was true in the past and q is true now. The statement captures the idea that "the now" moves over time, changing what is present.

Prior's temporal logic has had a significant impact beyond philosophy. It is used in computer science for the verification of programs and systems, in artificial intelligence for temporal reasoning, and in linguistics for the analysis of appearance and verb tense.

In the context of the study of the instant, temporal logic offers a rigorous formal framework for exploring the complexities of our temporal experience. It allows us to express and analyse with precision the relationships between the present moment, the past and the future, as well as more abstract concepts such as duration, simultaneity and temporal change. Quoting the Prior himself:

"The present is simply not a mere reference point... It is the source of all reality, from which time flows."[29]

In this quote, Prior is expressing a philosophical view known as "presentism", which maintains that only the present really exists. According to this perspective:

1. The present is not simply an arbitrary point on a timeline.
2. The present is ontologically fundamental – it is the basis of all reality.
3. Time is not a pre-existing dimension through which we move, but rather "flows" or emanates from the present.
4. Past and future do not have an independent existence, but are constructs based on the present.

This view contrasts with other theories of time, such as eternalism (which holds that past, present and future exist equally) or the theory of the block of the universe (which sees time as a static dimension).

Prior's quote emphasizes the centrality and importance of the present in our experience and understanding of reality and time. It suggests that our sense of time and reality is anchored in our immediate experience of the present, rather than in an abstract conception of time as a series of equivalent moments.

Finally, Gilles Deleuze, a twentieth-century French philosopher, offers us a revolutionary vision of time that questions our usual conceptions. To understand his ideas, we must begin by abandoning the image of time as a straight line and adopting instead the metaphor of the "rhizome"".

A rhizome, in botany, is a type of underground stem that grows horizontally, emitting roots and shoots from its nodes in all directions. Deleuze and his collaborator Félix Guattari They adopted this concept to describe systems of thought and, in our case, to rethink the nature of time and the instant.

We imagine time not as a river flowing in one direction, but as a vast subterranean field of rhizomes, stretching in all directions, creating unexpected connections, and gushing out at unpredictable points. In this view, each instant is not a fixed point on a line, but a node in this complex and constantly expanding network.

When we experience an instant, according to Deleuze, we are not simply occupying a point in time. We are activating a node in this rhizomatic network, making connections to the past and the future in unpredictable ways. For example, when we remember a past event, we are not simply accessing a fixed point in our memory. We are creating a new connection in the temporal rhizome, potentially altering both our understanding of the past and our experience of the present and our expectations for the future.

This rhizomatic conception of time leads us to Deleuze's idea of "becoming" rather than "being". Just as a rhizome is always in the process of growth and transformation, never in a fixed state, Deleuze sees the instant not as a static moment, but as a dynamic process of change and creation. As he writes in "Difference and Repetition":

"Time is no longer the circle of movement, but the spiral of becoming."[30]

In this model, time does not move in a single direction or at a uniform pace. Just as a rhizome can have multiple simultaneous growth points, Deleuzian time has multiple coexisting "presents," each with its own connections and potentialities. This idea calls into question the notion of a single universal present and opens up the possibility of diverse and overlapping temporalities.

The non-hierarchical structure of the rhizome also reflects Deleuze's resistance to totalizing explanations or the "grand narratives" of time. There is no "main trunk" of time from which everything is derived. Instead, there are a multitude of timelines intersecting, bifurcating, and reconnecting in unpredictable ways.

This view has important implications for how we understand events and causality. An event, in Deleuze's perspective, is not simply something that happens at a given moment. It is rather a convergence of multiple timelines, a point of intensity in the rhizomatic network of time. Each event brings with it the potential to reconfigure the entire network, creating new connections and opening up new possibilities.

Deleuze also makes us rethink our own relationship with time. We are not external observers of the temporal flow, but an integral part of this rhizomatic network. Our consciousness, our identity, is constantly being formed and reformed through the connections we make and the timelines we activate. As he writes in "Logic of Sense":

"It is not time that is in us, it is we who are in time."[31]

This rhizomatic conception of time and the instant opens up new possibilities for creativity and novelty. Each instant, as a node in this complex network, contains the potential for unexpected connections and creations. We are not simply moving along a predetermined path, but constantly creating new routes and connections.

Ultimately, Deleuze's view of time directs us to a new way of thinking and experiencing our temporal existence. It leads us to see beyond the seemingly smooth and predictable surface of time, and to immerse ourselves in its rhizomatic depths, always changing and creative. By doing so, Deleuze suggests, we can open ourselves up to new ways of thinking, creating, and existing in the world.

2.2. The tension between subjective perception and objective existence

THIS SECTION WILL EXPLORE the complex relationship between how we subjectively experience the instant and how it is objectively considered in scientific and philosophical terms.

Our understanding of the instant lies at a crossroads between subjective experience and objective descriptions of time. This tension is fundamental to understanding the ontology of the instant.

2.2.1. The phenomenological experience of the instant

FROM A SUBJECTIVE POINT of view, the instant is presented as an immediate and lived experience. Phenomenologically, it seems to have a certain duration, however brief it may be. When we say "now," that "now" seems to extend beyond a mathematical point with no extension.

Edmund Husserl (1859-1938), in his analyses of the consciousness of internal time, proposed concepts such as "retention" and "protention"[32] to explain how we experience the present. According to Husserl, the lived present is not a point, but a temporal field that includes an immediate past and an anticipated future. In his "Lessons in the Phenomenology of the Inner Consciousness of Time", Husserl writes:

"The concrete present... it is not a mere point of objectivity, but is in itself an extended objectivity."[33]

This perspective suggests that our subjective experience of the instant is inherently richer and more complex than a purely punctual conception, since:

A. Temporal extension: The present is not instantaneous, but has a certain temporal "width".

B. Complex structure: This extended present includes not only the immediate now, but also retentions of the recent past and tendencies towards the immediate future.

C. Continuity of experience: This conception helps explain how we experience time as a continuous flow rather than a series of discrete moments.

D. Objectivity: By calling it an "extended objectivity", Husserl suggests that this structure of the present is not merely subjective, but has a certain objective reality.

WILLIAM JAMES (1842-1910) introduced the concept of "specious gift", suggesting that our perception of the present has a certain amplitude, typically several seconds. In "The Principles of Psychology", James states that:

"Knowledge of any other fragment of the [consciousness] stream, past or future, near or remote, is always mixed with our knowledge of the present."[34]

This idea of the specious present indicates that our subjective experience of the instant is not a precise cut in the flow of time, but a window of variable duration. From his famous metaphor of the "stream of consciousness" James is arguing that our conscious experience is not a series of discrete states, but a continuous flow where the present is always intertwined with the memory of the past and the anticipation of the future.

To finish this section, we will mention the work of Maurice Merleau-Ponty (1908-1961) where he delves into the embodied nature of our temporal experience. In his "Phenomenology of Perception", he argues that:

"The lived present contains in its thickness a past and a future that extend without limit." [35]

This vision emphasizes how our perception of the instant is deeply rooted in our bodily existence and our interaction with the world. When he speaks of the "thickness" of the lived present, he is asking us to imagine the present moment as something that has depth and density, rather than as a simple point in a timeline.

This density of the present, according to Merleau-Ponty, is constituted by the constant presence of the past and the future. It is not simply that we remember the past or anticipate the future while living in the present, but that these temporal elements are an integral part of our current experience. The past is not only what has been left behind, but continues to live on and influence our present. In the same way, the future is not simply what is yet to come, but is already present in the form of possibilities, expectations and projects that shape our current experience.

When Merleau-Ponty says that this past and future "extend without limit," he is suggesting to us that our experience of the present is not confined to a narrow time interval. Instead, all of our past and all of our future possibilities are potentially present in every moment we live. This does not mean that we are constantly aware of all our history or all our possible futures, but that these are always available, forming the horizon of our present experience.

This view of time is intimately linked to Merleau-Ponty's broader philosophy of perception and embodied existence. For him, our experience of the world is always mediated by our body and placed in a specific context. In the same way, our experience of time is not that of a neutral observer looking at an objective clock, but that of an incarnated being who experiences time from within.

The implications of this perspective are important. He argues that our identity and our understanding of the world are not based on a series of discrete moments, but on a continuous and rich temporal experience. Memory is not simply an archive of the past, but an active part of our present experience. In the same way, our expectations and future projects are not simply abstract plans, but elements that shape how we live in the current moment.

This vision of time also calls into question the more objective or scientific conceptions that treat time as a measurable and uniform dimension. For Merleau-Ponty, time lived is qualitatively different from clock time. It is flexible, subjective and deeply linked to our bodily experience and our situation in the world.

2.2.2. Scientific models of time and the instant

IN CONTRAST TO THESE subjective experiences, scientific and mathematical descriptions of time tend to conceive of the instant as a point with no duration in a continuous timeline.

In classical physics, time is treated as a continuous dimension, where instants are infinitesimal points. Isaac Newton (1643-1727) conceived of time as absolute and independent of the observer. In his "Principia Mathematica", Newton writes:

"Absolute, true and mathematical time, by itself and by its very nature, flows uniformly without relation to anything external."[36]

This Newtonian conception presents the instant as a precise point in an objective and universal timeline.

Albert Einstein's theory of relativity (1879-1955) further complicated this view, showing that simultaneity is relative to the observer. In special relativity, the notion of a universal instant dissolves, since simultaneous events in one frame of reference may not be simultaneous in another. Einstein stated that:

"The distinction between past, present and future is only an illusion, albeit a persistent one."[37]

This relativistic perspective profoundly questions the notion of an objective and universal instant, and reflects Einstein's view of time as a dimension in a four-dimensional space-time continuum, where past, present, and future exist simultaneously. This idea, known as "eternalism" or "blog universe''", stands in stark contrast to our everyday experience of time as a flow from the past to the future through the present.

In quantum mechanics, Werner Heisenberg's uncertainty principle (1901-1976) suggests fundamental limits to the precision with which we can measure time on very small scales. Heisenberg argues that:

"What we observe is not nature itself, but nature exposed to our method of interrogation."[38]

This idea introduces a fundamental ambiguity into the notion of instant at the subatomic level, further blurring the line between subjectivity and objectivity. This sentence contains a fundamental idea in the interpretation of Copenhagen of quantum mechanics, of which Heisenberg was one of the main proponents. It reflects the notion that in the quantum world, the act of observation or measurement inevitably affects what is being observed. Some key points about this quote are:

1. Subjectivity in science: It suggests that our understanding of nature is inevitably influenced by the methods and instruments we use to study it.

1. Limits of knowledge: It implies that there are inherent limits to our knowledge of "objective" reality.

2. Observer-observed relationship: In quantum mechanics, the observer cannot be completely separated from the observed system.

3. Philosophy of science: Raises profound questions about the nature of scientific knowledge and the relationship between theory and reality.

2.2.3. Reconciliation of subjective and objective perspectives

THE TENSION BETWEEN these subjective and objective perspectives of the instant raises ontological questions that have generated several attempts at reconciliation.

Henri Bergson (1859-1941) argued that the true nature of time can only be grasped through direct experience, and that scientific descriptions, while useful, do not capture the essence of lived time. In his work "Duration and Simultaneity", Bergson writes:

"Science cannot deal with time without converting it into space and without applying the idea of measurement, which is spatial. Pure and simple experience knows neither measure nor space."[39]

This perspective suggests that the instant, in its deepest reality, may be inaccessible to conventional scientific methods. Thus, we see here a direct criticism of science: Bergson argues that science, in its attempt to understand time, transforms it into something that can be measured and quantified, essentially turning it into a spatial dimension. Other relevant aspects would be:

a. Time vs. Space: For Bergson, there is a fundamental distinction between real time (which he calls "duration") and space. Science, according to him, treats time as if it were space.

b. Pure experience: Bergson argues that our direct and immediate experience of time (the "pure duration") is qualitatively different from the scientific conception of time.

c. Limits of measurement: It suggests that the act of measuring time inevitably distorts it, since measurement is essentially a spatial concept.

d. Critique of homogeneous time: Bergson opposes the idea of a uniform and measurable time, arguing that this is an abstraction that moves away from the real experience of time.

In conclusion, Bergson underlines the importance of lived experience and the qualitative nature of time understood as "duration".

ON THE OTHER HAND, philosophers such as Bertrand Russell (1872-1970) have defended a more objectivist view, arguing that our subjective experience of time can be misleading and that we should rely on more rigorous scientific descriptions. This perspective suggests that the instant, as an ontological entity, can be better understood through mathematical and physical models than through subjective experience.

An interesting attempt at reconciliation comes from naturalized phenomenology, an approach that seeks to integrate phenomenological perspectives with cognitive sciences. Francisco Varela (1946-2001), in his work on neurophenomenology, proposes:

"The mind is nowhere to be found, and it is in this sense that cognition and the world arise together."[40]

This view suggests that the instant could be understood as a co-emergence of subjective experience and objective neural processes. This hypothesis raises the following implications:

1. Reality of the instant: The tension between subjective experience and objective description raises the question of whether the instant is a real entity or simply a useful construct for our understanding of time.

2. Limits of Knowledge: This discussion points to the potential limits of our knowledge about the nature of time and instant. Can it be that certain aspects of the instant are inaccessible to both subjective and objective experience?

3. Integration of perspectives: The tension between

subjectivity and objectivity in the understanding of the moment suggests the need for an integrated approach that can incorporate both lived experience and scientific descriptions.

4. Ethical and existential implications: The way we conceive of the instant, whether as a subjective experience or as an objective reality, can affect the way we understand our existence and how we make ethical decisions.

5. New research directions: This tension opens up new avenues for interdisciplinary research, inviting collaboration between philosophers, cognitive scientists, physicists, and other disciplines to address the complex nature of the instant.

In conclusion, the relationship between subjective perception and the objective existence of the instant continues to be one of the central challenges in the ontology of time. This tension is not only a theoretical problem, but it is crucial for our understanding of reality, consciousness and our own existence in time.

2.3. Theories of time and their influence on the conception of the instant.

THE WAY WE CONCEIVE of time has a direct impact on our understanding of the instant. The various theories of time that have developed throughout the history of philosophy and physics offer different perspectives on the nature of the instant, its reality, and its relationship to the past and the future.

In this section, we will explore three major dichotomies in theories of time: presentism versus eternalism, theory B of time in contrast to other conceptions, and the cyclical versus linear view of time. Each of these theoretical perspectives provides a unique insight into the ontology of the instant and its philosophical and scientific implications.

2.3.1. Presentist vs. Eternalist Theories

AT THE HEART OF THE philosophy of time, we find a fundamental debate between two apparently irreconcilable perspectives: presentism and eternalism. This discussion is not merely academic; It has profound implications for our understanding of reality, the nature of change and, crucially, the conception of the instant.

Presentism maintains that only the present exists. According to this view, the past is no longer real and the future is not yet. The only thing we can consider genuinely existent is the present moment. This perspective is strongly related to our everyday experience of time. When we say "now", we feel that we are pointing to something unique and fleeting, a reality that constantly slips through our conceptual fingers.

Proponents of presentism[41] argue that this theory offers a simpler and more intuitive explanation of temporal reality. They argue that it best captures our sense of the passage of time and the temporal "tension" we all experience. Moreover, presentism seems to align well with the notion of an open and undetermined future, leaving room for free will and contingency.

However, presenteeism is not without objections. How can we, for example, account for the truth of statements about the past if it no longer exists? And how can we understand causality if the past events that supposedly cause the present are no longer real? These problems have led many philosophers to look for alternatives.

This is where eternalism comes into play. This theory proposes that past, present and future exist equally. From this perspective, all moments of time are equally real. The instant, instead of being the only reality, simply becomes one more point in a static timeline.

An important author who defends eternalism is J.M.E. McTaggart, especially known for his work on the philosophy of time. McTaggart argues that time, as we normally conceive of it (in terms of past, present, and future), is unreal. In his work *The Unreality of Time* (1908), McTaggart divides time into two main series:

-**Serie A**: This is the traditional perspective of time, in which events are classified as past, present, or future. This perspective is constantly changing, as what is present becomes the past, and the future becomes the present. According to McTaggart, the A-series implies a contradiction because events constantly pass through the three categories, which he considers incoherent.

-**Serie B**: This perspective does not classify events in terms of past, present, or future, but as fixed before and after relationships. Events are permanently ordered in a timeline, and do not change their position in relation to other events. For example, the year 2000 will always be prior to 2020, with no change in this relationship. According to McTaggart, this is the only coherent way to think about time, as it does not involve the contradictory changes of the A-series.

In short, the **B series** represents an eternalist view of time, where all events are fixed in a timeless temporal structure, and there is no continuously changing "present", as is the case in the A series:

"The distinctions of past, present, and future are essential to time, but they involve contradictions, and therefore time cannot be real."[42]

Eternalism finds a foothold in Einstein's theory of special relativity, which questions the idea of a universal present. If simultaneity is relative to the observer, how can we speak of an objective "now"? In addition, eternalism offers an elegant explanation of how claims about the past and future can be true, and provides a solid foundation for understanding causal relationships and the persistence of objects over time.

Finally, we must not confuse eternalism with the theory of eternal return. Eternalism, as described by McTaggart's B-series, does not imply that events repeat themselves eternally. Instead, it suggests that all events exist in a fixed way in time, in a permanent temporal structure. This means that past, present, and future events already "exist" somewhere in the timeline, but they don't "repeat" or "happen again." Each event is fixed and does not repeat itself endlessly. For example, according to this view, the year 2000 is not repeated in loops, but simply occupies a fixed position in time. From the eternalist perspective, time is more like a movie, where all events are recorded once and for all, and an observer could "see" any moment from different perspectives. Thus, events do not change or repeat themselves, but are always permanently ordered in the timeline, without the need to happen again and again. Therefore, eternalism does not imply repetition of facts, but a fixed co-existence of all events in the timeline, where the "change" or "flow" of time is an illusion of our consciousness.

J.J.C. SMART, ANOTHER prominent proponent of theory B of time, argues that the passage of time is an illusion and that only temporal extension is real. According to this view, our sense of a mobile present is a characteristic of our experience, not of the physical world.

Despite its theoretical elegance, eternalism also faces difficulties. For example, how can we explain our profound subjective experience of the passage of time if all moments exist equally? And what implications does this view have for the concept of free will, if all events, including our future acts of will, already "exist" in some sense?

The tension between presentism and eternalism illustrates how different conceptions of time can lead to radically different visions of the nature of the instant and temporal reality in general. In presentism, the instant acquires a unique and privileged ontological status. In eternalism, the instant becomes one more point in a broader temporal structure, without special ontological privilege.

Summarizing:

- Face-to-face: Only the present is real. The past and the future do not exist.

- Eternalists: Past, present and future all exist at the same time. All the time is real.

- Theory B: Time is a series of ordered moments, all equally real, without privileging any of them as the "present".

2.3.2. Cyclic Time vs. Linear Time

WHEN WE THINK OF TIME, we often imagine it as a straight line that stretches infinitely into the past and the future. This is the linear conception of time, deeply rooted in modern Western thought. But it is not the only way to conceive of time. Throughout history and in various cultures, there has been another alternative vision: that of cyclical time.

The idea of linear time is familiar to us. It is the notion that events happen in an irreversible sequence, from the past to the present and into the future. Each moment is unique and unrepeatable. This vision is closely linked to the idea of progress, so central to Western thought since the Enlightenment. It implies that history has a direction, that we are moving towards some kind of future, be it better or worse.

On the other hand, the cyclical conception of time suggests that events repeat themselves in cycles. This idea is present in many ancient cultures and in some Eastern philosophies. In this view, time is not a straight line, but rather a circle or spiral. Events, epochs, perhaps even lives, repeat themselves in an eternal pattern.

The cyclical conception of time can be found in various forms. In Hinduism and Buddhism, for example, there is the idea of "samsara", the cycle of birth, death and rebirth. In ancient Greece, philosophers such as the Stoics spoke of "eternal recurrence", the idea that the universe repeats itself in infinite cycles.

Even in modern Western thought, the idea of cyclical time has had its proponents. Friedrich Nietzsche, for example, explored the idea of the "eternal return", suggesting that if time is infinite and instead the force and matter of the universe are finite, inevitably all events would repeat themselves infinitely. Let's analyze this Nietzschean argument in detail:

1. Premise 1: The force in the universe is finite

    This is a metaphysical assumption that is obviously not verifiable, but it is possible that it is based on the idea that the total energy (or "force") of the universe is limited. According to the laws of thermodynamics, energy is neither created nor destroyed, it is only transformed. If we accept that the total amount of energy in the universe is finite, this premise may be reasonably tenable from a scientific perspective.

2. Premise 2: Time is infinite.

    This premise presupposes that time will continue indefinitely without an end, a hypothesis that, from a cosmological point of view, is debated. However, if this statement is accepted as valid for the argument, it places us in a situation where time continues indefinitely while energy (force) is finite.

3. Premise 3: The combinations of force to generate experiences are finite

    Here, the argument assumes that the ways in which energy can combine in the universe to create events or phenomena is limited. This is a speculative statement that could be disputed, but if we consider it in a finite universe of resources, particles, forces and physical laws, it may make sense. The number of possible combinations of particles and energies would be limited, especially if we assume a deterministic universe, where physical laws determine how these forces are organized.

4. **Conclusion: Finite combinations in infinite time will be repeated**

This conclusion correctly derives from the above premises. If the set of combinations is finite and time is infinite, all possible combinations must be repeated, because there are no more new ways to combine force. This is the heart of the idea of eternal return: the infinite repetition of the same events or configurations.

5. **Additional conclusion: Everything will be repeated infinitely many times**

This statement is the last conclusion of the reasoning and seems coherent within the proposed scheme. If the combinations are finite and time is infinite, they will not only be repeated once or many times, but they will be repeated an infinite number of times.

Critical analysis

- Simplification of physical reality: The plot assumes a universe with stable conditions (where the physical laws and conditions of the universe do not change over time). However, some cosmological models suggest that the universe could undergo irreversible changes, such as thermal death or indefinite expansion, which could prevent this infinite repetition of events.

- Philosophical implications: Nietzsche uses the eternal return not only as a cosmological hypothesis, but also as an existential reflection. Your argument, although coherent from a logical point of view, is rooted more in physical speculation than in the ethical and personal dimension that Nietzsche wanted to explore with this concept.

Conclusion

The argument is coherent within its own logic, as long as we accept the initial premises. However, the applicability of this reasoning depends on whether or not we consider valid the claims about the finitude of force and the infinity of time, which are unproven ideas and depend on cosmological hypotheses that are not yet fully resolved by science. Likewise, it does not contemplate possible irreversible changes in the universe that could break this infinite repetition.

Be that as it may, Nietzsche's theory of eternal return defends the idea of the eternal instant, not because it never ends (which would make it impossible for other instants, other events to appear) but because it repeats itself endlessly.

As we can see, these different conceptions of time have decisive implications for how we understand the instant. In a linear vision, each moment is unique and irrecoverable. Once it has passed, it will never return. This can give every moment a sense of urgency and importance.

In a cyclical view, on the other hand, each instant could be seen as part of a pattern that repeats itself. This idea could lead to a different perspective on life and our actions. If everything is going to happen again and again, what is the meaning of what we are doing now?

It is important to note that these views are not necessarily mutually exclusive. Some cultures have combined elements of both. For example, in some interpretations of Mayan thought, time is conceived as cyclical in a broad sense, but with a linear progression within each cycle.

In modern physics, the question of whether time is cyclical or linear takes on new dimensions. Some cosmological models suggest the possibility of a cyclic universe, which expands and contracts repeatedly. Other theories, such as the accelerated expansion of the universe, seem to point more towards a linear view.

The tension between these two conceptions of time continues to influence how we think about the past, present and future. It affects how we understand history, how we value our actions in the present and how we imagine the future.

Ultimately, the way we conceive of time—whether as a straight line or as an eternal cycle—has profound implications for how we understand our life and our place in the universe. It influences how we give meaning to our lives and how we deal with the big questions of existence, change and permanence.

2.4. The instant from the perspective of modern physics

MODERN PHYSICS HAS revolutionized our understanding of time and, by extension, of the instant. The theories developed throughout the twentieth and early twenty-first centuries radically question our everyday intuitions about the nature of time.

The theory of special relativity published in 1905, was the first major earthquake in our conception of time. Einstein showed that time is not absolute, but depends on the observer's frame of reference. This means that two observers in relative motion with respect to each other will experience the passage of time differently. This phenomenon, known as time dilation, has been experimentally confirmed numerous times.

But what does this mean for the moment? In special relativity, the idea of a universal instant, a "now" that is the same for all observers of the universe, simply does not exist. What is simultaneous for one observer may not be so for another. This implies that the instant, as we intuitively conceive it, loses its absolute character.

The theory of general relativity, published by Einstein in 1915, goes further. It shows us that time is intrinsically linked to space, forming a continuum called space-time. The presence of mass and energy curves this space-time, affecting not only the movement of objects, but also the flow of time itself. Near very massive objects, such as black holes, time flows more slowly than in deep space.

In this context, the instant becomes an even more elusive concept. We can no longer speak of a universal instant, but of events in space-time. The separation between space and time, so clear in our everyday experience, is blurred in the equations of general relativity.

Quantum mechanics, the other great revolution in physics of the twentieth century, provides an even more disconcerting perspective on the instant. In the quantum world, Heisenberg's uncertainty principle sets fundamental limits on how accurately we can measure certain pairs of physical properties, such as the position and momentum of a particle, or energy and time.

This principle suggests that, at very small scales, the concept of instant loses meaning. We cannot speak of a precise moment in which a quantum event occurs. Instead, we have an overlap of possibilities that resolves only when a measurement is taken.

More recently, theories that attempt to unify general relativity and quantum mechanics, such as string theory and loop quantum gravity, have proposed even more radical ideas about the nature of time and instant. Some of these theories suggest that time could be an emergent, not fundamental, property of the universe. Others propose that at smaller scales, time could be discrete, composed of indivisible "quanta of time". To sum up, we can mention three current references of these theories:

Carlo Rovelli and loop quantum gravity: Carlo Rovelli is one of the leaders in the theory of Loop Quantum Gravity (LQG). This theory proposes that spacetime is discrete at small scales, such as Planck's length, and suggests that time might not be critical, but an emergent property of more basic interactions. Rovelli's book *Quantum Gravity* (2004) explores these concepts in depth. [43]

Lee Smolin and the idea of discrete time: Lee Smolin has contributed a lot to quantum gravity and has extensively discussed the possibility of time and space being discrete. In his book *Three Roads to Quantum Gravity* (2001), Smolin discusses the quantum nature of space-time and how it might be composed of "quanta" at small scales.[44]

Edward Witten and string theory: Edward Witten, one of the most prominent theorists in string theory, has discussed the possibility of time and space emerging from more fundamental structures, such as strings. In his article "Reflections on the Fate of Spacetime" (1996), published in *Physics Today*, mentions these ideas about the nature of space-time.[45]

It should be noted that many of these ideas are still speculative and are within the limits of our current knowledge. However, what is clear is that modern physics forces us to rethink our conception of the instant. Far from being an unambiguous point in a universal timeline, the instant is revealed as a complex and relative concept. Depending on the frame of reference, it is intertwined with space, but at smaller scales, it fades into a haze of quantum uncertainty.

2.4.1. Relativity and the relativity of simultaneity

EINSTEIN'S THEORY OF special relativity (1905) revolutionized our understanding of time and space. One of his most surprising and counterintuitive concepts is the relativity of simultaneity.

In classical Newtonian physics, it was assumed that if two events were simultaneous for one observer, they would be simultaneous for all observers, regardless of their motion. Einstein proved that this is not true.

The relativity of simultaneity states that two events that are simultaneous in one frame of reference may not be simultaneous in another frame of reference that moves with respect to the first. In other words, simultaneity is not absolute, but relative to the observer's frame of reference.

To understand this, let's imagine a classic example:

Suppose we have a long train moving at high speed. In the middle of the train there is an observer. Exactly at the moment when the center of the train passes in front of an observer who is on the platform, two flashes of lightning occur, one at each end of the train.

For the observer of the platform, if the light of the two lightning strikes reaches him at the same time, he will conclude that the lightning strikes were simultaneous, since he is equidistant from the two points where they occurred.

However, for the observer inside the train, the situation is different. As the train is in motion, this observer moves towards the light coming from the front lightning and away from the light from the rear lightning. Therefore, it will see first the light of the front lightning and then that of the rear, concluding that the lightning was not simultaneous.

Both observers are right from their own frame of reference. There is no "correct" or privileged frame of reference.

This relativity of simultaneity has great implications for our conception of the instant. It suggests that there is no universal "now" that is the same for all observers of the universe. What is "now" for an observer may be "before" or "after" for another observer in relative motion.

This fact contradicts our intuition of an absolute time and a universal instant. In relativity, the instant becomes a local concept, dependent on the observer's frame of reference.

It is important to note that these effects are only significant at speeds close to the speed of light. In our everyday experience, where the relative speeds are much lower, the difference in simultaneity is so small that we do not notice it. This explains why our Newtonian intuition of time works well in daily life, despite not being strictly correct.

The relativity of simultaneity is more than a theoretical curiosity. It has practical implications in technologies such as GPS, where relativistic effects must be taken into account to obtain adequate accuracy.

In short, the relativity of simultaneity shows us that the instant, far from being an absolute and universal concept, is relative and dependent on the observer, which forces us to rethink our conception of time and reality itself.

2.4.2. Quantum mechanics and temporal indeterminacy

QUANTUM MECHANICS, developed in the first half of the twentieth century, offers a vision of the world radically different from classical physics. One of its most intriguing aspects is how it treats time and, by extension, the instant.

The uncertainty principle by Heisenberg[46], a fundamental pillar of quantum mechanics, has profound implications for our understanding of time. This principle states that there are fundamental limits to the precision with which we can simultaneously measure certain pairs of physical properties, such as the position and momentum of a particle.

A lesser-known but equally important version of this principle concerns energy and time. It establishes that:

$\Delta E * \Delta t \geq \hbar/2$

Where ΔE is the uncertainty in energy, Δt is the uncertainty in time, and $\hbar$ is Planck's constant Reduced.

What does this mean for the moment? It suggests that, at very small scales, we cannot define a precise instant for a quantum event if we want to know precisely the energy involved. The more precisely we try to determine when an event occurs, the more uncertain the energy involved becomes, and vice versa.

This temporal indeterminacy has the following implications:

1. Diffuse instant: At the quantum level, the instant becomes "diffuse". We cannot speak of a precise

moment in which a quantum event occurs.

1. Quantum fluctuations: In very short time intervals, the energy of a system can fluctuate significantly due to this indeterminacy.
2. Virtual particles: This indeterminacy allows the existence of so-called "virtual particles" that can appear and disappear in very short intervals of time.
3. Tunnel effect: Phenomena such as the quantum tunneling effect, where a particle can cross a barrier that would classically be impenetrable, are possible thanks to this temporal indeterminacy.

In addition, in quantum mechanics, time is treated differently than in classical physics. While in classical mechanics time is an external parameter that marks the evolution of a system, in quantum mechanics time is integrated into the Schrödinger wave equation[47], which describes the evolution of quantum states.

Another aspect to consider is the concept of quantum superposition. A quantum system can exist in a superposition of different states until a measurement is made. This fact raises relevant questions about the nature of the instant: when does a quantum event actually occur? At the time of superposition or at the time of measurement?

The Copenhagen Interpretation[48], one of the most widely accepted interpretations of quantum mechanics, suggests that a quantum system does not have defined properties until a measurement is made. This fact could imply that the instant at which a quantum event occurs is not well defined until we interact with the system.

It is important to note that these ideas are counterintuitive and test our classical conception of time and the instant. However, quantum mechanics has proven to be an extremely accurate and successful theory in its predictions.

In short, quantum mechanics and temporal indeterminacy show us that, at the smallest scales of reality, the instant loses its precise definition. It becomes a fluid and probabilistic concept, calling into question our classical intuition of a continuous and objectively defined time.

2.4.3. Theories of Quantum Gravity and Discrete Time

THEORIES OF QUANTUM gravity They try to reconcile two fundamental pillars of modern physics: the theory of general relativity and quantum mechanics. This reconciliation is one of the great challenges of contemporary physics, and the proposals that have emerged have decisive implications for our understanding of time and the instant.

One of the most surprising ideas that have emerged from some approaches to quantum gravity is the possibility that time is discrete at extremely small scales, rather than continuous as we experience it in our everyday lives.

Loop Quantum Gravity (LQG)[49] is a theory that seeks to combine quantum mechanics with Einstein's general relativity, to explain gravity at the quantum scale, that is, how gravity works at very small levels, such as inside black holes or just after the Big Bang. He defends the existence of a minimum unit of time, often called "Planck time". This would be the shortest time interval that would make physical sense, approximately 10^{-44} seconds. To put this figure into perspective, it is much shorter than the time it takes for light to pass through the nucleus of an atom.

What would a discreet time imply for our understanding of the instant?

1. There would be no instants "between" these quanta of

time. The instant would become an indivisible unit, like a pixel in a digital image.

1. The flow of time could be conceived as a succession of these discrete instants, like the frames of a film.
2. The notion of an infinitesimally small "now" would lose meaning. The "now" would have a defined minimum duration.
3. Zeno's paradoxes, like that of the arrow, could be resolved in this framework: the movement would occur in minimal discrete "jumps".

In addition to discrete time, other quantum gravity proposals suggest even more radical ideas:

- Emergent time: Some theories propose that time is not fundamental, but emerges from more basic structures at the quantum level.[50]

- Space-time overlay: In analogy with quantum superposition, some models suggest that superpositions of different space-time geometries could exist.[51]

- Quantum causality: The classical notion of causality could be modified at quantum scales, affecting our understanding of time succession.[52]

These ideas radically test our intuition about time and the instant. They suggest that our experience of time as a continuous flow could be a macroscopic approximation of a much more complex reality and alien to microscopic scales.

In short, theories of quantum gravity, in their attempt to reconcile general relativity with quantum mechanics, offer us radically new insights into the nature of time and instant. The idea of discrete time, in particular, represents a challenge to our intuitive conception of time and opens up new avenues for understanding the fundamental structure of reality.

2.5. Mathematical analysis of the instant

THE MATHEMATICAL ANALYSIS of the instant leads us to consider how mathematics conceptualizes time and, in particular, how it models a point in time. This analysis is critical not only for pure mathematics, but also for theoretical physics and other disciplines that rely on mathematical models of time.

In mathematics, the instant is typically conceptualized as a point on a line that represents time. This line is modeled as a continuum, specifically as the set of real numbers. Each real number corresponds to an "instant" in this model.

This representation has several important implications:

- **Continuity**: Time is considered continuous. Between any couple of instants, there are always infinite intermediate instants.

- **Density**: There are no "gaps" in time. Any interval of time, no matter how small, contains infinite instants.

- **Order**: The instants have a defined order, corresponding to the order of the real numbers.

- **Measurability**: We can assign a "distance" between two instants, which corresponds to the numerical difference between them.

Differential and integral calculus, developed by Newton and Leibniz, provides us with powerful tools to work with this conceptualization of the instant. A key concept in this context is that of **limit**, which allows us to understand what happens when we get closer and closer to a specific moment.

Understanding limits intuitively

We can think of the concept of limit as the idea of getting closer to a particular point in a function as the variable approaches a certain value, although the function does not necessarily have to take that value at the point. For example, if we want to know what the exact speed of a car is at a precise time, we need to use the concept of **instantaneous speed**. Average speed is defined as the distance traveled divided by the total time taken to travel it, but instantaneous speed refers to the speed at a specific time, which is calculated by the limit of the average speed when the time interval tends to zero.

If we measure the distance traveled in smaller and smaller intervals of time, we will obtain average velocities closer and closer to the instantaneous velocity at that point. The limit allows us to formalize this idea: it helps us find the exact speed in an instant when we consider time intervals that tend to zero. Although we cannot directly measure the speed at a precise moment due to practical limitations, we can calculate what this speed would be thanks to the limit, which offers us a rigorous tool to describe the behavior of a system when the time interval becomes infinitely small.

Application of limits in differential calculation

Differential calculus studies the rate of change of a function in relation to a variable. The derivative is a mathematical tool that allows us to calculate the instantaneous rate of change of a function, that is, how fast something is changing at a specific time.

Returning to the example of the car, the derivative tells us what its speed is at a precise instant, based on how its position varies as the time interval tends to zero. Thus, although an instant has no duration, the concept of limit allows us to talk about how things are changing at that moment considering smaller and smaller intervals of time.

Limits in integral calculus

Integral calculus is complementary to differential calculus. If differential calculus tells us how things change in an instant, integral calculus allows us to add up the effects of these changes over a time interval to obtain a cumulative result. While differential calculus deals with instantaneous rates of change, integral calculus adds infinitesimally small quantities to obtain a total measure.

For example, if we want to know what total amount of water has entered a tank during a period in which the flow rate varies constantly, we cannot simply multiply the average flow rate by the total time. Instead, we divide the time into very small intervals and add up the amount of water that enters each of these intervals. This sum is an approximation of the total amount, but as the time intervals get smaller, our sum gets closer to the actual value. The limit of this infinitesimally small sum is what we call the definite integral, which gives us the exact total value.

Resolving the paradox of moments without duration

An interesting question that arises is: how can an infinite set of instants without duration form an interval of time with finite duration? The answer lies in the fact that, although each instant individually has no duration, the continuous set of infinite instants along an interval generates a totality with finite duration.

We can imagine it as a continuous line formed by an uncountable infinity of points. Although no single point has length, the infinite density of points along the line results in a definite length. Similarly, an interval of time is made up of an infinite uncountable set of instants, and although no instant has duration, the interval as a whole has a finite measure.

Other mathematical perspectives on the instant

Non-standard analysis: This branch of mathematics uses the concept of infinitesimals, which are infinitely small but non-zero numbers. These quantities are smaller than any positive real number, but they are not exactly equal to zero. Non-standard analysis allows us to work with ideas of change and movement at an infinitely small scale more intuitively, offering a rigorous alternative to traditional limit-based calculus.[53]

Temporal logic: It is a framework that allows us to reason about the temporal relationships between events without the need to quantify time precisely. With operators such as "always" or "eventually", temporal logic is especially useful for understanding the order of events and is widely used in computer science to analyze the correct execution of dynamic programs and systems.[54]

In theoretical physics, especially in some theories of quantum gravity, it is proposed that time and space could be discrete at very small scales, such as the Planck scale. This means that, at fundamental levels, space-time could be made up of indivisible units, similar to pixels on a screen, but immensely small.[55] These ideas require new mathematical tools, such as space-time networks or spin graphs, and challenge our traditional understanding of time as a continuum.

Conclusion

The mathematical analysis of the instant provides us with an in-depth understanding of how we can work with the concept of time in mathematics and science. Using ideas such as limits, infinitesimals, temporal logic and discrete theories of physics, we are able to describe how things change at precise moments and how these changes accumulate over time. At the same time, these perspectives lead us to reflect on the nature of time and the instant, exploring the subtleties and paradoxes that arise in these fundamental concepts.

3. THE PARADOX OF THE ETERNAL INSTANT: PERCEPTION OF THE PRESENT IN A WORLD OF CONTINUOUS FLUX

While we have previously explored the concept of the present as an isolated instant, in this chapter we will delve into an even deeper paradox: the notion of the eternal instant. This concept goes beyond mere temporary isolation; It suggests an experience where the present seems to expand infinitely, transcending the conventional limitations of time.

The eternal instant is not simply a moment disconnected from the flow of time, but an experience where the present seems to contain within itself all eternity. This idea calls into question not only our understanding of time as a sequence of instants, but also our conception of the relationship between temporality and eternity.

In contrast to the previous analysis of the isolated instant, here we will explore:

1. The unique subjective experiences associated with the perception of the eternal instant, including altered states of consciousness and mystical experiences.

1. How this concept has manifested itself in various artistic expressions, offering a cultural and creative perspective that complements previous philosophical and scientific analyses.
2. The implications of this paradox for our understanding of consciousness, exploring how the experience of the eternal instant can illuminate aspects of the human mind that go beyond mere temporal perception.
3. Modern neuroscience perspectives on these experiences, seeking to understand how the brain can generate the sensation of a present that seems to embrace eternity.

This exploration seeks to delve into the experiential and cultural dimensions of our relationship with time, complementing and expanding the more theoretical and philosophical analyses that we have previously carried out. In doing so, we hope to gain a richer and more multifaceted understanding of how humans perceive and conceptualize the present in a universe characterized by constant change.

3.1. Conceptualization of the eternal instant

THE ETERNAL INSTANT is presented as a notion that contrasts with our usual understanding of time. This concept refers to a singular experience where the present moment acquires a quality of infinity, transcending the conventional boundaries of time. It is not simply an isolated moment, but an experience where the present seems to expand to embrace the whole of existence.

The idea of the eternal instant has captivated the attention of thinkers and mystics throughout history. Plato, in his dialogue "Timaeus", spoke of an "eternal now", describing it as a moving image of eternity.[56] Centuries later, in Christian mysticism, figures such as Meister Eckhart They recounted experiences where time and eternity seemed to converge at a single point.[57] Eastern traditions have also explored similar concepts; in Buddhism and Hinduism, states of consciousness such as "satori" or the "samadhi" are described as moments that transcend the ordinary perception of time.

In the modern era, philosophers such as Henri Bergson have brought new perspectives to this ancient idea. Bergson introduced the concept of "pure duration", an experience of time that escapes quantitative measurement and that is qualitatively distinguished from the chronological time that governs our daily lives.

The notion of an eternal instant carries with it an obvious paradox: how can something be both momentary and eternal? How can a single instant contain or reflect the totality of time? These questions are not mere exercises in logic; They point to the limitations of our language and conceptual thinking to capture certain experiences of consciousness that seem to transcend the usual categories of time and duration.

This conceptualization of the eternal instant forces us to reconsider the distinction we often make between temporality and eternity. It suggests the possibility of an experience of time radically different from our everyday perception, where the present, past and future merge into an indivisible unity. At the same time, it raises questions about the nature of consciousness and its relationship with time.

In exploring this concept, we do not necessarily seek to resolve these paradoxes. Rather, we use them as a starting point to deepen our understanding of temporal perception and human consciousness.

Conclusions:

1. The eternal instant is not simply a philosophical curiosity, but a phenomenon that points to a possible discontinuity in the nature of time and consciousness.

2. The existence of reported experiences of an eternal instant suggests that human consciousness may operate in temporal modes different from the usual linear, indicating a little-explored cognitive flexibility.

3. The convergence between subjective experiences of the eternal instant and certain modern physical theories suggests that our everyday perception of time

may be a simplification of a much more complex temporal reality.

4. The concept of the eternal instant highlights the need for a new conceptual and linguistic framework for describing and analysing non-linear temporal experiences.

5. The study of the eternal instant could provide valuable insights into the relationship between the brain, consciousness and time, opening up new avenues of research in cognitive neuroscience.

3.2. Experiences of the eternal instant

THE EXPERIENCES OF the eternal instant have been reported in various contexts, from spiritual practices to extreme situations. These experiences are characterized by a profound alteration in the perception of time, where the present seems to expand to embrace a sense of eternity.

1. Mystical and religious experiences.

William James, in his influential work "The Varieties of Religious Experience" (1902), documents numerous instances of mystical experiences involving an altered perception of time. A particularly vivid example is J.A. Symonds' account:
"Suddenly, in a moment, time seemed to have stopped... Infinity entered me with a sudden wave... I felt that I had arrived at the plastic reality of existence... The entire universe seemed to have become a pure timeless crystal."

1. Altered states of consciousness.

Modern research on altered states of consciousness has provided empirical evidence of similar experiences. Roland Griffiths et al., in a study published in "Psychopharmacology" (2006) on psilocybin-induced mystical experiences, collected the following testimony:
"Time came to a complete standstill. I felt that I was out of time and space as we know them... It was as if everything that had happened and everything that would happen was contained in that moment."

1. Near-death experiences (NDEs):

NDEs often include accounts of a radically altered perception of time. Pim van Lommel, in "Consciousness Beyond Life" (2010), quotes the testimony of a patient who experienced cardiac arrest:

"I experienced the beginning and the end of the universe and everything in between... Everything was happening at once, and I was everything and I was everywhere."

1. Situations of high stress or danger:

Already in the nineteenth century, the geologist Albert Heim He documented unusual temporary experiences in mountaineers who had survived severe falls. In "Notizen über den Tod durch Absturz" (1892), he quotes:

"The time was enormously extended... Thoughts and images followed one another with the speed of light... Everything seemed cheerful and beautiful, without pain or anxiety."

1. Deep meditation:

Meditative practices often lead to experiences of temporary disruption. Jack Kornfield, in "A Path with Heart" (1993), describes:

"Suddenly, time stopped. There was no past or future, only an eternal present... Every breath, every sensation, seemed to contain all eternity."

1. Artistic experiences:

Even in everyday contexts, some individuals report similar experiences. Virginia Woolf, in "A Sketch of the Past" (1939), describes:

"Suddenly, something happened... Time stands still. The current moment is full to overflowing... That's when I receive... a shock; At that moment I had a revelation of some real existence behind the appearances."

Modern neuroscience has begun to investigate the neural correlates of these experiences. A study by Marc Wittmann et al., published in "The Journal of Neuroscience" (2011), suggest:

"The activation of the anterior insula correlates with the subjective duration of time... suggesting a crucial role of this region in the perception of duration and awareness of the present moment."

These various sources of evidence allow us to affirm that the experience of the eternal instant is not an isolated phenomenon, but a latent capacity of human consciousness that can emerge in various circumstances. The variety of contexts in which these experiences are reported – from deep meditation to situations of extreme danger – indicates that they could be related to fundamental mechanisms of consciousness and temporal perception.

3.3. The eternal instant in artistic creation

THE NOTION OF THE ETERNAL instant has inspired and tested artists from various disciplines throughout history. This section will explore how different art forms have attempted to capture or evoke the experience of the eternal instant.

1. Visual arts:

Painting and photography have often sought to capture moments that seem to transcend time. For example, the surrealist painter Salvador Dalí he explored the distortion of time in works such as "The Persistence of Memory" (1931). Dalí commented on this work:

"The soft distortion of my soft watch at the time of the first explosion in Hiroshima has petrified time forever."[58]

In photography, Henri Cartier-Bresson coined the term "decisive moment", describing it as:

"The simultaneous recognition, in a fraction of a second, of the meaning of an event as well as of a precise organization of forms that give that event its appropriate expression." (Henri Cartier-Bresson, "The Decisive Moment", 1952)

1. Literature:

Many writers have tried to capture the essence of the eternal instant in their prose and poetry. James Joyce, in "Ulysses" (1922), uses the stream of consciousness to create moments that seem to contain eternities. In an interview, Joyce said:

"In the universal particular, the eternal 'now', all the past and all the future are included." (James Joyce, interview with Arthur Power, 1922)

1. Music:

Composers with John Cage have explored the relationship between sound, silence and the perception of time. In his famous piece "4'33"" (1952), Cage creates a framework for experiencing the immediate present. Cage wrote:

"There is nothing like silence. What they thought was silence, because they didn't know how to listen, was full of accidental sounds." (John Cage, "Silence: Lectures and Writings", 1961)

1. Dance and performance:

The choreographer Pina Bausch He often creates pieces that play with the perception of time. In an interview, he commented:

"There are moments on stage where time seems to stand still. It is as if all the past and all the future are contained in this instant." (Pina Bausch, interview with Der Spiegel, 1990)

1. Cinema:

Directors such as Andrei Tarkovsky have explored the manipulation of time in cinema. In his book "Sculpting in Time", Tarkovsky writes:

"What is a film if not 'fixing time'? Time fixed in its forms and factual manifestations: this is the supreme concept of cinema as art." (Andrei Tarkovsky, "Sculpting in Time", 1986)

These various artistic expressions of the eternal instant share some common themes:

1. The tension between the specific moment and eternity.

1. The attempt to capture or evoke an experience that goes beyond normal temporal boundaries.
2. The use of techniques specific to each medium to alter the viewer's perception of time.

The artistic exploration of the eternal instant not only reflects intense subjective experiences, but also makes us rethink our conventional conceptions of time and reality. Through art, we are proposed to live, even if only momentarily, a temporal perspective that transcends our daily experience.

3.4. Time, Consciousness and Reality

TIME IS A PARADOX THAT slips through our fingers, an intangible presence that orders the universe but at the same time seems to be an illusion created by the mind. Consciousness is the internal space where this illusion unfolds, the theater where moments are represented and the notion of reality is constructed.

If time is the canvas and consciousness is the painter, reality could be the ever-evolving work that emerges from this interaction. Perhaps the past, present and future are nothing more than conventions, reference points on a map that we draw as we progress. The line that separates the objective from the subjective becomes blurred when we realize that temporal perception can vary according to mental state, emotions or experiences.

These reflections open the door to a new understanding of the world, a perspective where time, consciousness and reality are intertwined threads of the same tapestry. And it invites us to question the nature of what we consider real and to explore the depths of human experience without the limitations of conventional structures.

3.4.1. The Eternal Instant and Theories of Consciousness

THE STUDY OF THE ETERNAL instant opens up new perspectives on the nature of consciousness and our perception of reality. This phenomenon, which seems to transcend the normal constraints of time, raises fundamental questions about how we experience and interpret the world around us.

In the field of theories of consciousness, the eternal instant presents itself as an intriguing challenge. David Chalmers[59] He considers it part of the "difficult problem" of consciousness, questioning how a physical process in the brain can generate an experience so radically different from our usual perception of time. This perspective suggests that the eternal instant could be a key to understanding the relationship between brain processes and subjective experience.

Integrated Information Theory by Giulio Tononi[60] offers a possible explanation. According to this theory, experiences of eternal instant could represent states of consciousness with a high degree of informational integration, where multiple aspects of the experience merge into a coherent unity. This idea proposes that the eternal instant is not an anomaly, but an extreme manifestation of the integrative capacities of consciousness.

When we consider free will and determinism, the eternal instant acquires an unexpected relevance. The studies of Benjamin Libet[61] on decision-making have shown that brain activity often precedes awareness of the decision. However, the experience of the eternal instant suggests the possibility of a nonlinear interaction between consciousness and these neural processes. Daniel Dennett[62] He goes further, proposing that our ability to perceive time flexibly, including experiences such as the eternal instant, could be central to our sense of agency and free will.

Modern neuroscience is beginning to unravel the brain mechanisms behind these extraordinary temporary experiences. David Eagleman[63] concludes that "The brain does not record time in a linear way. The brain stores richer and more abundant information when we are faced with stressful or unknown events, producing the illusion that time has slowed down." This flexibility in temporal processing could explain, in part, the experience of the eternal instant.

The studies of Olaf Blanke[64] Experiences outside the body have revealed that alterations in the activity of certain brain regions, particularly the temporoparietal junction, can cause sensations of disembodiment and temporal alteration. These findings suggest a neural basis for experiences that transcend our normal perception of time and space.

Anil Seth[65], with his perceptual prediction approach, proposes that the eternal instant could arise when the brain's predictions about time flow are broken. This would result in an "extended present" experience", where the usual limits of the present moment seem to dissolve.

These scientific perspectives, far from demystifying the eternal instant, place it as a key phenomenon for understanding the mechanisms of consciousness and the neural construction of our temporal experience. The integration of these ideas with philosophical reflections and artistic expressions offers us a richer and more nuanced view of the nature of consciousness and reality.

The study of the eternal instant, therefore, is not just a philosophical question, but a window into the depths of the human mind and its relationship with time and reality. As we advance in our understanding of this phenomenon, we are likely to gain new insights into the nature of consciousness, free will, and our subjective experience of the world.

3.4.2. Relationship with the concepts of free will and determinism

LET'S IMAGINE FOR A moment that we are immersed in the experience of an eternal instant. Time seems to stand still, and in this dilated space, the possibilities open up before us like an infinite fan. It is in this context that the relationship between the eternal instant and the notions of free will and determinism takes on a new dimension.

Alfred Mele, a contemporary philosopher, proposes that we consider how this expansion of temporal perception could influence our ability to make decisions. In his book "Free", Mele [66] It raises an interesting question: if our sense of time can expand in this way, could it not then offer us a wider opportunity for conscious reflection and deliberation? This idea opens up the possibility that, in these moments of perceived eternity, our autonomy will be strengthened, allowing us to consider our choices with unusual depth.

But what if we live in a deterministic universe? This is where the compatibilist perspective comes into play. We imagine the eternal instant not as an escape from determinism, but as a state of consciousness that amplifies our "graduated freedom", as Daniel Dennet puts it. In this state, we may not escape the causal laws of the universe, but we experience the maximum degree of freedom that these laws allow.

Shaun Gallagher[67] leads us to consider an even deeper dimension. What if these intense temporal experiences were crucial to our ability to be moral agents? Gallagher suggests that moments like the eternal instant are not mere anecdotes, but experiences that shape our ability to respond ethically to the world around us.

Finally, Raymond Tallis[68] It offers us a vision that almost seems like science fiction. Let us imagine that the eternal instant is not just an alteration of our perception, but an indication of a unique capacity of human consciousness: the ability to transcend the limits of the immediate present. Tallis proposes that this ability to "get out of time" could be the very basis of our freedom, allowing us to mentally explore possible futures and alternative pasts.

Thus, the eternal instant is revealed not only as a controversial experience, but as a window into the depths of human consciousness and its relationship with time and freedom. It forces us to rethink what it means to be free, what it means to make a decision, and how our experience of time shapes our ability to act in the world, within the intricate dance of the flow of time.

3.4.3. Neuroscience Perspectives on the Perception of Time and the Eternal Instant

IN THE LABYRINTHS OF the human brain are hidden the secrets of how we perceive time, and among them, perhaps the key to understanding the enigmatic eternal moment. Neuroscientists, armed with their sophisticated brain imaging tools and computational models, delve into this mysterious territory, seeking to unravel the mechanisms that underlie our temporal experience.

Imagine yourself now walking through the corridors of a modern neuroscience laboratory. In each room, researchers in white coats bend over complex apparatus, all with a common goal: to unravel the mysteries of how our brains perceive time.

In one of these rooms, we find Dean Buonomano, from the University of California. With an enthusiastic smile, he explains his revolutionary theory. "You see," he says, pointing to a screen full of undulating patterns, "the brain doesn't have a central clock like we thought before. Instead, it uses these patterns of neural activity to measure time, like waves in a lake after throwing a stone." His eyes sparkle as he speculates: "Perhaps, in an eternal instant, these neural waves behave in unusual ways, creating the sensation of an infinitely expanding present."

Crossing the Atlantic, we find ourselves in the laboratory of Moshe Bar at Harvard. Bar greets us with an intriguing question: "What do you think will happen in the next few seconds?" Before we can answer, he continues, "Your brain is already making predictions about this. It constantly generates 'pre-feelings' about the immediate future." He pauses dramatically before adding, "But what happens when these predictions fail completely? Maybe that's what happens in an eternal instant."

Our journey continues in Japan, where Ryota Kanai it greets us with a 3D model of the brain slowly spinning on a screen. "Look at this," he says, pointing to different regions that light up. "Awareness of time could emerge from how the brain integrates information at different scales." His eyes light up as he speculates: "An eternal instant could be a unique state of information integration, an extraordinary neural synchrony."

Finally, we return to Europe to meet Marc Wittmann. Instead of a conventional laboratory, it takes us to a quiet room with meditation cushions. "The key," he says softly, "could be in how we perceive our own body." It invites us to close our eyes and concentrate on our heartbeat. "Notice how your perception of time changes when you focus on your body? Imagine this amplified a thousand times. Maybe that's what an eternal moment feels like."

As we emerge from this imaginary journey through the laboratories of the world, we realize that the eternal instant, far from being an unattainable mystery, is slowly being unraveled by these passionate scientists. Each theory, each experiment, is one more piece in the great puzzle of how our brain constructs our experience of time.

And who knows? Perhaps at some point, in some laboratory, someone will be able to capture the neural essence of an eternal instant, opening new doors to the understanding of human consciousness and our perception of reality.

3.4.4. Language and the Perception of Time: The Plot of "Arrival"

THE SCIENCE FICTION film "Arrival" (2016), inspired by the short novel *The story of your life*, by Ted Chiang, and directed by Denis Villeneuve, explores an interesting connection between language and the perception of time. The central premise of the story is that learning a non-linear alien language can alter the way the brain perceives and experiences time, allowing for simultaneous insight into the past, present, and future.

In the film, linguist Louise Banks is recruited to communicate with aliens who have arrived on Earth. As he deciphers his complex and circular visual language, he begins to have visions of the future. Eventually, he realizes that alien language, free of the temporal linearity of human languages, has rewired his brain to perceive time in a non-linear way.

This concept of "Arrival" has its roots in the linguistic relativity hypothesis, also known as the Sapir-Whorf hypothesis[69]. According to this theory, the language structures we use affect our cognition and the way we perceive and conceptualize the world. In the extreme case posed in "Arrival", a radically different language could alter something as fundamental as our experience of time.

Although the premise of "Arrival" is speculative, it leads us to reflect on the relationship between language, thought and perception. Could a language structured in a nonlinear way engender a nonlinear perception of time? And conversely, to what extent do our languages, with their essentially sequential organization, condition our ordinary temporal experience?

Certainly, human languages have ways of evoking a certain timelessness or eternity, either through timeless nouns ("truth," "beauty") or the timeless present of proverbs and general truths ("the sun rises in the east"). But in general, they are profoundly marked by temporality and sequentiality, with their verb tenses and the linearity of syntax and narrative.

However, some philosophical and spiritual traditions have sought to transcend the limitations of language to point to a reality beyond time. The Taoist philosopher Zhuangzi speaks of a "language without words" and a "discourse without discourse" to evoke the Tao eternal and ineffable. And certain forms of mystical poetry, such as Zen haikus or Sufi poetry, try to evoke an eternal moment beyond words.

Therefore, while the idea of a language that allows for a non-linear perception of time remains speculative, "Arrival" reminds us of the power of language to shape our experience and proposes us to explore the limits and possibilities of our forms of temporal expression. Ultimately, it may be that the eternal instant, like the Tao, resides not in a particular language, but in the silences and intervals that dwell between words.

4. THE UNDERSTANDING OF THE ETERNAL INSTANT IN BUDDHISM AND MEDITATIVE PRACTICES.

THE ETERNAL INSTANT in Buddhism Transcends the mere temporal notion to become a direct manifestation of the ultimate nature of reality, as conceived in Buddhist philosophy. This concept is deeply related to fundamental ideas such as *Sunyata* (empty), *pratityasamutpada* (dependent origination) and *tathata* (such).

Sunyata [70], or emptiness, is an essential concept within Buddhism that denotes the inherent lack of existence of all phenomena. This is because no phenomenon has its own or independent essence; everything exists depending on multiple causes and conditions. Understanding *sunyata* is crucial to getting rid of attachment and suffering, as it reveals that no object or experience has a fixed nature, and that everything is inevitably interrelated.

Pratityasamutpada, or dependent origination, is the principle that all phenomena exist only in relation to other phenomena. Nothing exists autonomously, but each phenomenon is conditioned by other factors. This concept shows us that reality is an interdependent network in which each element influences and is influenced by the others. In this context, the understanding of *pratityasamutpada* provides a basis for understanding *sunyata*: the lack of inherent existence (*sunyata*) is a direct consequence of the interdependence of all things (*pratityasamutpada*). These two concepts, seen together, are fundamental to understanding the nature of causality and to achieving liberation through the recognition of universal interconnectedness.

The *tathata*, or suchness, refers to "reality as it is" or the "essential nature of things". This term describes the quality of perceived reality without the distortions imposed by the conceptual mind. It is the pure and inherent nature of all phenomena, seen without judgment or illusion. In Mahayana Buddhism, suchness represents the direct understanding of reality as it is, beyond appearances and mental projections.[71]

To better understand the concept of *tathata* or "suchness", we can use a simple example. Let's say you're looking at a tree. Usually, when we look at a tree, we immediately assign it a label: "this is an oak tree", "it is very tall", "it has green leaves", etc. These are the projections of our conceptual mind: we add judgments, labels, and interpretations that we have learned throughout our lives. *Tathata* refers to experiencing the tree as it is, without adding any interpretations to it. It is simply witnessing the tree, without defining it, without categorizing it, and without the preconceived ideas we usually have about trees. It is perceiving the tree in its purest state, without mental interference.[72] Ultimately, it implies an intuitive union with the essence of the tree, within the framework of a non-dual consciousness.[73]

The eternal instant is not simply a prolonged moment, but the realization of the illusory nature of linear time. That is, the eternal instant is not simply a point in time that lasts indefinitely. It's not that time stops or stretches forever. Rather, it refers to the understanding that linear time, as we normally experience it (as a sequence of past, present, and future events), is a construct of our mind. The idea of the eternal instant is that, when these mental constructions are transcended, one can experience a reality in which linear time ceases to make sense. It is a direct experience of reality, beyond the limitations of the past and the future, where there is only the present moment, which is perceived as the totality of reality. This experience is associated with a deeper awareness of the nature of reality, as is the case in advanced meditation in Buddhism.

According to the *Sutra del Lankavatara* [74], a key text of Mahayana Buddhism, the perception of time as a succession of events is a construction of the *Vijnana* (conditioned mind), which is the way in which our consciousness, under the influence of conditioning, processes the phenomenal world. In contrast, the eternal instant refers to the direct experience of the *jnana* (non-dual consciousness) [75], which transcends this artificial fragmentation of time. The *jnana* it is a state of perception in which the conventional divisions between subject and object, between the observer and the observed, are dissolved. In this state, reality is perceived as an indivisible unity. This experience of non-dual consciousness allows one to see reality without the limitations imposed by the conditioned mind, thus freeing oneself from the fragmented and distorted perception of the world.

The eternal instant, therefore, is the experience of a reality free from the limitations of linear time, in which all phenomena are perceived as interrelated and lacking intrinsic existence. This experience constitutes the core of the practice of Mahayana Buddhism, which leads us to understand that time and space are not absolute realities, but relative constructions created by the conditioned mind.

4.1. Meditative Practices in Buddhism: Portals to the Eternal Instant

MEDITATIVE PRACTICES in Buddhism transcend simple relaxation or concentration; They are profoundly sophisticated methodologies for the investigation of the nature of the mind and reality, including our perception of time and the eternal instant. These practices differ according to the various Buddhist schools, but they all converge on the common goal of achieving an immediate understanding of the ultimate nature of existence.

1. Samatha and Vipassana Practices

SAMATHA (CALM) AND Vipassana (penetrating vision) constitute two essential practices in multiple Buddhist traditions [Kornfield, 1993].

Samatha is aimed at developing one-point concentration, a quality that allows the meditator to experience states of pure consciousness, where the perception of temporal flow disintegrates. In complete absorption into the object of meditation (usually the breath), the meditator comes to a conventional time-wasting experience, in which the sense of timelessness emerges strongly.

Vipassana, on the other hand, involves the development of a meticulous awareness of sensations, thoughts, and emotions that continually arise and dissolve. This practice reveals the transitory and insubstantial nature of mental and physical phenomena. Through observation of the arising and cessation of each experience in the present moment, the meditator comes to discern the illusory nature of linear time and to experience the timeless quality of pure consciousness.

2. Zazen and Shikantaza Practices

WITHIN THE FRAMEWORK of the Zen tradition, especially in the Soto school, the practice of zazen (seated meditation) and, in particular, shikantaza ("just sit") constitute direct manifestations of the eternal instant.

Shikantaza, as taught by Master Dogen, is not a technique to reach a specific state, but the direct expression of inner enlightenment. This view is based on Dogen's teachings, especially his text *Shobogenzo* [Dogen, 1240][76]. In this practice, the meditator simply sits without any particular goal or focus, embodying the fullness of each moment. This is what Dogen calls "uji" or "being-time", where each instant embodies the totality of existence.

3. Dzogchen and Mahamudra Practices

IN THE VAJRAYANA TRADITION of Tibetan Buddhism, the advanced practices of Dzogchen and Mahamudra They provide direct methods for recognizing and resting on the primordial nature of the mind.

In Dzogchen, the practice of "trekchö" ("cutting through") involves breaking all mental constructs to reveal the naked nature of consciousness, which is timeless and not dual. This practice is documented in the classical texts of Dzogchen, such as the *Kunje Gyalpo* [Norbu, 1996]. The practice of "tögal" implies the integration of this vision into all experiences, perceiving each phenomenon as a manifestation of the primordial basis.

Mahamudra, on the other hand, uses a series of progressive meditations that lead the practitioner to recognize the nature of the mind as clear light, transcending the limitations of time and space. In the Mahamudra state, past, present and future are perceived simultaneously in a timeless instant.

4. Koan

WITHIN THE RINZAI ZEN tradition, the practice of koan is a unique method of dismantling the limitations of conceptual thinking and directly experiencing reality beyond time.

A famous koan, as it is:

"What was your original face before your parents were born?"

challenges common notions about time and causality. This question is part of the collection of koans known as the *Mumonkan* [Mumon, 1228]. The resolution of a koan is not an intellectual response, but a direct experience that transcends linear temporality.[77]

5. Compassion Meditation and Tonglen

ALTHOUGH IT MAY SEEM less related to the eternal instant, compassion meditation, especially the Tibetan practice of Tonglen ("give and receive"), also facilitates a profound experience of timelessness. This practice is described in detail by Pema Chödrön in her book *The Places That Scare You* [Chödrön, 2001].

In Tonglen, the practitioner visualizes taking on the suffering of others with the inhalation and sending happiness and well-being with the exhalation. This practice dissolves the barriers between self and other, as well as between past, present, and future, leading to an experience of timeless interconnectedness.

6. Meditation on Impermanence

MANY BUDDHIST TRADITIONS emphasize meditation on impermanence as a fundamental means of understanding the illusory nature of time and existence itself. In Buddhism, impermanence is one of the three hallmarks of reality, along with suffering and the non-existence of a permanent self. This understanding is essential for freeing the mind from the attachments and illusions that lead to suffering.

Through the constant practice of meditation, the practitioner learns to observe with mindfulness how all phenomena, both internal and external, are in a state of perpetual change. Thoughts, emotions, bodily sensations, and external events appear and disappear like clouds in a changing sky. This direct observation of transience allows the meditator to realize that clinging to what is impermanent only generates dissatisfaction and suffering.

As the practice deepens, the meditator comes to perceive the incessant flow of the eternal present that underlies all apparent changes. This experience of the eternal "now" reveals that the past has already passed and the future has not yet arrived, and that the only tangible reality is the present moment. By recognizing this, anxieties about the future and regrets about the past are dissolved, allowing for a fuller, more conscious existence.

Moreover, this deep understanding of impermanence helps to dispel illusions about a fixed and immutable self. By seeing that all the parts we consider as "me" are also subject to change, we can release the ego and cultivate greater compassion and empathy towards all beings. In this way, meditation on impermanence not only transforms the perception of time, but also leads to a profound personal and spiritual transformation. As an example, in the Dhammapada, one of the most important texts of the Pali canon, which collects sayings and teachings attributed to the Buddha, we find this quote:

"All conditioned phenomena are impermanent. When one sees it wisely, one dissociates oneself from suffering. This is the path of purification."

5. ETHICS OF THE INSTANT

In the constant flow of human experience, each moment presents an ethical crossroads. The decisions we make in these fleeting, seemingly insignificant moments weave the tapestry of our moral behavior. The ethics of the instant, therefore, is not just an abstract philosophical reflection, but an exploration of how we navigate the moral terrain in real time.

Our perception of the present, shaped by psychological, cultural, and now technological factors, profoundly influences how we approach ethical decisions. In a world where immediacy seems to reign supreme, where decisions often have to be made in fractions of a second, the question of how to maintain a moral compass becomes increasingly urgent.

This chapter sets out to examine the intersection between our experience of the present time and our ethical choices. We will explore how the pressure of the instant can distort our moral judgment, how immediate perceptions can influence our ethical decisions, and how the digital age, with its constant demand for attention and immediate response, is reshaping the landscape of ethical responsibility.

Through this exploration, we will seek to understand not only how the immediate present conditions our ethical decisions, but also how we can develop an ethic that is capable of responding nimbly to the immediate demands of each situation, while remaining faithful to enduring ethical principles.

In doing so, we may discover that in the ethics of the moment it is not just about making quick decisions, but about developing a conscious presence that allows us to act with integrity even under the pressure of immediacy.

Ultimately, this chapter makes us consider how we can live ethically not only in the long term, but in each present moment, recognizing that it is in these fleeting moments that our moral essence is truly manifested.

5.1. Ethical Decisions in the Present Moment

IN AN EMERGENCY OPERATING room, a surgeon is faced with a critical decision. Time seems to stand still as he considers options that could save or endanger the patient's life. At this moment, their perception of time and their experience of the present play a crucial role in their ethical decision.

This scene brings us to the heart of the question: how does our perception of the present influence our immediate ethical decisions?

El Dr. Shauna Shapiro and colleagues explored this relationship in a study published in "The Journal of Positive Psychology". They found that mindfulness practices, which intensify our awareness of the present moment, can significantly improve our moral reasoning and ethical decision-making. As Shapiro explains:

"The practice of mindfulness appears to broaden the window of awareness, allowing participants to perceive more information and consider multiple perspectives before making a decision."[78]

This "window of consciousness" can expand dramatically into experiences of eternal instant. Psychologist William James described those moments when "a small period of time may seem infinitely long" (James, "The Principles of Psychology", 1890). A New York firefighter recounted a similar experience after 9/11, describing how time seemed to stand still, allowing him to consider all options before making a crucial decision.

However, in the digital age, our experience of the present is changing rapidly. Nicholas Carr, in his book "The Shallows" [79], argues that the constant immersion in the flow of digital information is profoundly altering our capacity for attention and reflection. Carr introduces the concept of a "reactive ethics" as opposed to a "reflective ethic":

"When we are constantly connected, we lose our ability to be reflective and introspective. Our ethics become reactive rather than reflective." (Carr, 2010)

Carr suggests that this transition to a more reactive ethic may have significant implications:

1. Impulsive decisions: We could make ethical decisions without fully considering their ramifications.

1. Moral inconsistency: Our ethical responses might vary more depending on the immediate context, rather than being based on consistent principles.
2. Vulnerability to manipulation: We may be more susceptible to external influences on our ethical decisions.

This observation raises questions about how digital culture is reshaping our experience of the present and, by extension, our capacity for immediate ethical deliberation.

The different philosophical conceptions of the instant also influence how we approach ethical decisions. As we have seen above, some philosophers conceive of the instant as an indivisible point in time, while others propose more fluid and continuous visions of time. These diverse perspectives can have a significant impact on how we understand and approach ethical decisions in the present moment. For example, a conception of the instant as part of a continuous flow could encourage a broader consideration of the consequences of our actions, while a view of the instant as an isolated point could emphasize the importance of immediate decision.

Ultimately, our ability to make ethical decisions in the present moment is intimately tied to how we experience that present. Whether through contemplative practices, eternal instant experiences, or navigating the challenges of the digital age, our perception of time shapes our immediate ethics. If the action subsequently deserves a moral or legal judgment, its assessment will vary depending on the temporal criterion chosen (discrete or continuous).

As we continue to explore the relationship between perception of the present and ethics, we face another challenge: how can we cultivate a fuller and more conscious presence in the digital age? How can we create spaces for deep ethical deliberation in the midst of the constant flow of information and immediate demands? Answering these questions can be key to enriching our capacity for ethical action in every moment we live.

5.2. The influence of immediate perception on moral judgment

LET'S IMAGINE OURSELVES in a busy metro station. Suddenly, we see a person falling onto the tracks just as the train is approaching. In a matter of seconds, we must decide whether to risk our lives to save it. This scenario, although extreme, illustrates how immediate perception can profoundly influence our moral judgments.

Psychologists Joshua Greene and Jonathan Haidt They have studied extensively how immediate emotions and intuitions influence our moral judgments. In his article "How (and where) does moral judgment work?" (2002), argue:

"Many moral judgments are caused by quick and automatic emotional responses, and not by conscious moral reasoning." [80]

Greene conducted experiments using functional magnetic resonance imaging to study how the brain processes moral dilemmas. He found that when people are faced with personal and emotionally charged moral dilemmas, the areas of the brain associated with emotion are activated more than the regions associated with abstract reasoning.

A classic example is the "tram dilemma"". When presented in abstract terms (diverting a tram to save five people at the expense of one), most people find it morally acceptable. But when it is approached in a more personal way (pushing someone on the tracks to save five), many people judge it as unacceptable, even though the net result is the same.

This phenomenon illustrates how the immediacy and vividness of perception can drastically influence our moral judgments.

Paul Slovic, in her study "If I look at the mass I will never act" (2007), explored how immediate perception influences our response to humanitarian crises. It found that people are more likely to help when presented with an identifiable individual than when presented with statistics about large groups. Slovic argued:

"Our ability to feel is limited... As the number of victims increases, our feelings become saturated and we no longer scale the response adequately."[81]

This "compassion fatigue" demonstrates how our immediate perception can limit our ability to make appropriate moral judgments in complex situations.

On the other hand, psychologist Barbara Fredrickson She has studied how positive emotions can broaden our perception and, therefore, influence our moral judgments. In his article "The role of positive emotions in positive psychology" (2001), he argues that positive emotions can "expand an individual's momentary thought-action repertoire", leading to more flexible and creative moral judgments.[82]

This research raises crucial questions about the relationship between immediate perception and moral judgment. How can we balance immediate emotional responses with more thoughtful moral reasoning? How can we expand our "window of perception"" to make more informed and compassionate moral judgments?

In the digital age, where decisions often have to be made in fractions of a second, these issues are more relevant than ever. Constant exposure to images and information can saturate our capacity for moral response, leading to what the philosopher Zygmunt Bauman calls "adiaphoreization" - moral indifference to the suffering of others.

Ultimately, understanding the influence of immediate perception on moral judgment can help us develop strategies for more balanced and compassionate ethical decision-making, both in high-pressure situations and in our everyday lives.

5.3. Ethical Responsibility in the Age of Digital Immediacy

IN A WORLD WHERE A tweet can trigger a diplomatic crisis and an Instagram post can influence millions of people, ethical responsibility in the digital age takes on a new dimension of urgency and complexity.

Let's imagine for a moment in the situation of a social media manager of a large company. A false rumor about the company's flagship product begins to circulate online. In a matter of minutes, the story goes viral. The pressure to respond immediately is overwhelming, but the responsibility to verify information before reacting is equally crucial. This increasingly common scenario illustrates the central ethical dilemma of the digital age: the tension between immediacy and responsibility.

Sherry Turkle, in his book "Alone Together" (2011), argues that constant connectivity is changing not only how we interact, but also how we think about ourselves and our ethical duties. Turkle writes:

"We are shaped by the technology we use... We become especially receptive to technologies that appeal to our human vulnerabilities."[83]

When Turkle says "We are shaped by the technology we use," he is suggesting that the technological tools we use are not simply neutral instruments, but have a profound impact on how we think, feel, and behave. The idea is that technology not only helps us to do things, but also shapes the way we are and interact with the world.

For example, the constant use of smartphones has changed the way we manage our time, how we maintain social relationships, and even how we experience moments of loneliness or boredom. Technology not only facilitates certain actions, but also predisposes us to certain patterns of thought and behavior.

The second part of the sentence, "We become especially receptive to technologies that appeal to our human vulnerabilities," delves even deeper into this idea. Turkle suggests that we are particularly susceptible to adopting and being influenced by technologies that align with our deepest psychological needs and weaknesses.

Some examples of this could be:

1. Social networks that appeal to our need for social validation and fear of missing out (FOMO - Fear of Missing Out).

1. Online games that exploit our tendency to seek immediate rewards and our susceptibility to addiction.
2. Dating apps that capitalize on our need for connection and intimacy, but can also encourage objectification and constant comparison.
3. News platforms that take advantage of our attraction to negative or scandalous information.

In essence, Turkle is warning that technology is not simply a neutral tool, but can actively exploit our psychological vulnerabilities, thus shaping the way we think and behave in ways that may not always be healthy or ethical.

This perspective invites us to be more aware and critical in our relationship with technology, to consider not only what technology allows us to do, but also how it is shaping us as individuals and as a society.

This "configuration" by technology has great implications for our ethical responsibility. The immediacy of digital communication can lead to impulsive and poorly thought-out responses, with potentially serious consequences.

A notable example is the case of Justine Sacco, a PR executive who posted an insensitive tweet just before boarding an 11-hour flight. By the time he landed, he had become the No. 1 topic on X (formerly Twitter) worldwide, he had lost his job, and his reputation was in ruins. This incident, analyzed by Jon Ronson in his book "So You've Been Publicly Shamed" (2015), he illustrates how the immediacy of social media can amplify momentary errors in judgment with disproportionate consequences.[84]

On the other hand, digital immediacy also offers unique opportunities for positive ethical action. Let's think of movements like #MeToo or viral fundraising campaigns for humanitarian causes. These initiatives demonstrate how instant connectivity can mobilize resources and attention for important ethical causes in unprecedented ways.

However, this same capacity for rapid mobilization also poses ethical challenges. Ethan Zuckerman, in his article "New Media, New Civics?" (2014), warns of the dangers of what he calls "low-effort activism" or "slacktivism"[85]. He argues that the ease of participating in online causes can create an illusion of ethical action without real commitment or meaningful change.

Ethical responsibility in the digital age also extends to the management of personal information. As Helen Nissenbaum points out in "Privacy in Context" (2010)[86], our traditional understanding of privacy is being challenged by the interconnected and immediate nature of digital technologies. Every click, every "like", every share, has ethical implications that can be difficult to foresee at the moment of action.

In the face of these challenges, how can we cultivate an ethical responsibility that is both responsive and reflective? Luciano Floridi, in "The Fourth Revolution" (2014)[87], proposes the concept of "infoethics" -an ethics adapted to the information age. Floridi argues that we need to develop new ethical virtues suitable for a world where our actions in the digital sphere have real and immediate consequences.

Ultimately, ethical responsibility in the age of digital immediacy requires a delicate balance. We must be able to respond quickly when necessary, but we must also cultivate the capacity for reflective pause. We need to develop what we could call an "ethics of digital presence" – a constant awareness of the ethical implications of our online actions.

This new ethical paradigm not only involves being aware of the consequences of our digital actions, but also understanding how immediacy and constant connectivity are reshaping our perception of time, of the other and of ourselves. By doing so, perhaps we will be able to take on the ethical challenges of the digital age with more wisdom and compassion.

5.4 Strategies for quick ethical decisions

TIME PRESSURE IS A reality that we often face in our daily lives. When time is limited and we have to make quick decisions, our thought process can be affected. Instead of reflecting deeply on the options available, we may react instinctively, based on habits or intuitions. This can be useful in situations where immediate action is needed, but it can also lead to mistakes or actions that do not align with our ethical values.

For example, let's imagine an emergency doctor who has to attend to multiple patients in a short time. Under pressure, you may be tempted to overlook certain procedures to speed up care, such as not washing your hands between patients. While this saves time, it puts patients' health at risk and violates the ethical principles of the medical profession.

Temporal pressure can limit our ability to analyze the consequences of our actions. When we feel pressured, it is more difficult to consider how our decisions will affect others or whether they are in line with our moral principles. A student who has not had time to study for an exam may decide to cheat, despite knowing that it is an incorrect action. The urgency of the moment may cause him to overlook the ethical implications of his behavior.

To deal with these situations and ensure that we make ethical decisions even under pressure, we can adopt several strategies. One of the most effective is to be clear about our personal values. If we know what is important to us, we are more likely to act in a manner consistent with these principles, regardless of the circumstances. For example, if we value integrity, we are less likely to deceive or manipulate information, even when time is at a premium.

Another strategy is to establish ethical guidelines or protocols that guide us in making quick decisions. Many professions have codes of conduct that can serve as a reference in times of haste. A journalist, for example, can follow an ethical guide that tells him to always verify the sources before publishing a news story, thus avoiding the dissemination of false information even if this means not being the first to give the news.

Using key questions can also be very helpful. In moments of quick decision, asking ourselves questions such as "Can this action harm someone?" or "Am I acting according to my values?" can provide us with the necessary clarity to choose the most ethical option. For example, a company director who has to make a quick decision about layoffs may wonder how this will affect employees and whether there are fairer alternatives.

Preparation and training in simulated situations can improve our ability to respond ethically under pressure. Professionals such as pilots or firefighters carry out drills to be prepared for real emergencies. This allows them to react appropriately when they are in life-or-death situations.

Managing stress is critical to maintaining mental clarity. Techniques such as deep breathing, meditation or simply taking a few seconds to compose ourselves can make a difference in how we deal with a stressful situation. An executive before an important meeting can spend a few minutes calming down to ensure that they will make the best decisions.

In summary, while time pressure can make it difficult to make ethical decisions, there are ways to ensure that we are acting in accordance with our values. Keeping our principles clear, following ethical guidelines, asking ourselves key questions, preparing for hurried situations, and managing stress are all effective strategies that can help us. Remember that decisions made in an instant can have lasting repercussions, and that is why it is essential to devote the necessary attention to doing the right thing, even when time is limited.

6. AESTHETICS OF THE PRESENT

The "Aesthetics of the present or the instant" is a concept that arises from a contemporary sensibility, focused on the valuation of the immediate and the ephemeral. This artistic and philosophical perspective emphasizes the direct experience of the moment, without in-depth or planned analysis. It is a way of appreciating the world as it is presented, in its crudest and most spontaneous form, without ornaments or filters.

This aesthetic emerges in a context where speed and transience define a large part of our daily existence. We live in an era in which technology and social networks have accustomed us to a form of communication and expression that is instantaneous and often ephemeral. Images are captured, shared, and consumed in a matter of seconds, influencing the way we perceive reality and art. Instead of contemplating a work or an idea for a long time, the "Aesthetics of the Moment" leads us to immerse ourselves in the immediacy of experience, to value the present moment without worrying about the past or the future.

In this sense, there is a celebration of spontaneity and naturalness. Creations arising from this sensibility are often immediate, fresh, and capture life in its most authentic state. We have good examples in disciplines such as instant photography, live broadcasts or also in the way we share fragments of our lives through social networks.

The "Aesthetics of the Present" is, therefore, an invitation to live and create in the moment, to put aside static reflection to embrace pure and momentary experience. It is a response to a rapidly changing world, where beauty and meaning are often found in the most fleeting moments.

6.1. Aesthetic appreciation of the ephemeral and the beauty of the unrepeatable

THE AESTHETIC APPRECIATION of the ephemeral refers to a way of valuing and contemplating what is temporary, transitory and short-lived. Unlike other forms of artistic experience that seek permanence, solidity, or durability, this appreciation focuses on the beauty and significance of things that disappear, are constantly transforming, or only exist for a brief period of time. This aesthetic of the ephemeral is deeply rooted in the awareness of the transience of life and the world around us.

One of the main characteristics of the aesthetics of the ephemeral is the appreciation of what is unique and unrepeatable. These are moments that cannot be recreated or relived in exactly the same way, such as a flower that blooms and wilts, an instant of creative inspiration or a chance encounter. This appreciation gives the ephemeral a special meaning because, by being aware that it will not return, the observer or creator projects an intensity and emotional value that he or she might not experience with something more permanent.

In this context, the ephemeral is not seen as a loss or a lack, but as an opportunity for connection with the present moment. There is a form of beauty in the very experience of this change and disappearance, since it reminds the viewer or the creator of the human condition: always in motion, always changing, always temporary.

6.2. The ephemeral as a response to contemporary society

THE AESTHETIC APPRECIATION of the ephemeral can also be seen as a response to contemporary society, in which speed, constant change and temporality are fundamental. We live in a world where information is consumed quickly, where fashions and trends appear and disappear in a matter of days or weeks, and where technologies have accustomed us to forms of immediate and short-term expression. In this context, the aesthetics of the ephemeral adapt and reflect this modern lifestyle.

A clear example is the influence of social media and digital culture, where images and experiences are shared and consumed almost instantaneously. Photographs that disappear after 24 hours, short videos and ephemeral messages are part of an aesthetic that does not seek permanence, but the capture of the moment. Here, the ephemeral becomes an artistic expression in itself, where the value lies in its immediate impact, and not in its durability.

6.3. Nature and the Ephemeral: A Deep-Rooted Connection

IN MANY CULTURAL TRADITIONS, especially in Eastern philosophy, the ephemeral has long been appreciated as a source of beauty and spiritual depth. A classic example is Zen philosophy and Japanese culture, with its celebration of the ephemeral through the concept of *mono no aware*[88], which refers to the subtle awareness of the transience of all things and the gentle melancholy that this produces.

The contemplation of cherry blossoms (sakura) in Japan is a ritual that exemplifies this sensitivity. Cherry trees bloom briefly during spring, and their beauty lies precisely in this transience - the flowers wither and fall off, symbolizing the passage of time and the changing nature of life. Thus, the experience of its contemplation is intense and emotional, because it reminds us of the fragility and temporality of everything we love.

6.4. Ephemeral art and performance

THE AESTHETIC APPRECIATION of the ephemeral has also given rise to specific artistic movements, such as performance art and temporary installations. In these art forms, the value of the work lies precisely in the fact that it only exists for a limited period of time. Once the "performance" has been completed or the installation has been dismantled, the work disappears, remaining only in the memory of the spectators or in fragmentary documentation.

This type of art values the interaction between the work and the audience at a specific time, turning each act into a unique and unrepeatable experience. A good example is contemporary dance, where the movement of bodies can only be experienced at the moment it is performed. Likewise, many works of urban art, such as temporary interventions in public spaces or sand art, emphasize temporality as an essential part of their artistic proposal.

6.5. Temporality as an existential reflection

THE PERCEPTION OF TEMPORALITY, transience and the ephemeral can trigger a deep reflection on the human condition and the meaning of existence. This reflection goes beyond aesthetics and delves into philosophy, addressing fundamental questions about life, death, time and the meaning of our actions in a world where everything is transitory.

6.5.1 The Consciousness of Finitude

TEMPORALITY, BY DEFINITION, implies an end. Everything that begins must conclude, and this universal truth is one of the deepest sources of existential reflection. The awareness of finitude – the certainty that both life and experiences, relationships and even works of art are ephemeral – can generate a wide range of emotional and philosophical reactions.

From the existential anguish expressed by thinkers such as Heidegger, to the serenity and acceptance of the passage of time found in Eastern philosophy, the awareness of temporality confronts us with our own mortality and with the impermanence of everything we know. This thought, far from being merely bleak, can act as a catalyst for a fuller and more conscious life, because it reminds us of the need to appreciate the present moment and to give meaning to our actions.

One of the philosophers who has most deeply reflected on temporality is Martin Heidegger. In his work *Being and Time*[89], Heidegger addresses the question of human existence from the notion of *be for death* (*Breast zum Tode*). According to Heidegger, it is precisely the awareness of our own death that allows us to live authentically. Death is not just an event that happens at the end of life, but a constant possibility that shapes our existence.

Heidegger suggests that, by confronting our own finitude, we can come to live more authentically, freely and consciously choosing our actions instead of letting ourselves be dragged along by the inertia of everyday life. This form of authenticity, which arises from reflecting on temporality, drives us to take responsibility for our lives, to recognize the importance of each moment, and to live with a sense of purpose and urgency.

6.5.2. Existentialism and the creation of meaning

TEMPORALITY IS ALSO a central theme in existentialism, a philosophical current that emphasizes individual freedom, responsibility and the creation of meaning in a world without absolute values. Philosophers such as Jean-Paul Sartre and Albert Camus They addressed the question of how to find meaning in a temporary and often absurd existence.

Sartre argued that, in a world where God does not exist and, therefore, there is no pre-established meaning, human beings are free to create their own meaning[90]. This radical freedom, however, is accompanied by a great responsibility, because every decision we make defines who we are in a context of temporality. Temporality, thus, becomes the backdrop against which our lives are defined.

Albert Camus, for his part, explored the theme of the absurd, the tension between our search for meaning and the indifference of the universe. In works such as *The myth of Sisyphus*[91], Camus argues that, although life is essentially absurd due to its temporality and lack of intrinsic meaning, human beings can find a form of revolt and freedom in the acceptance of this absurdity. Temporality, in this sense, is not an obstacle to signification, but a condition that allows us to create our own vital narrative.

6.5.3. Temporality in Eastern Philosophy

REFLECTION ON TEMPORALITY is not exclusive to Western thought. In Eastern philosophy, especially in Buddhism and Taoism, temporality and impermanence are central aspects of the understanding of reality. Rather than seeing temporality as a threat or a source of distress, these traditions teach to accept impermanence as a fundamental part of life.

Buddhism, for example, teaches that all things are impermanent (*anicca*) and that attachment to material things, to people, or even to one's own identity, is the source of suffering[92]. Acceptance of temporality and the changing nature of all things leads to greater serenity and a deeper understanding of reality. This acceptance is not resignation, but an invitation to live with full awareness of the present, without clinging to the past or worrying about the future.

6.5.4. Ephemeral Art as an Existential Metaphor

THE LINK BETWEEN TEMPORALITY and existential reflection can also be clearly seen in ephemeral art, which is often presented as a metaphor for human life. Works of art that are deliberately created to disappear, such as Christo's installations[93] and Jeanne-Claude, remind us of the temporality of existence and the beauty inherent in what is temporary.

[94]

These works do not seek immortality or endurance, but celebrate the beauty of the process and the moment. When the public contemplates an ephemeral work, they are forced to reflect on their own relationship with time and on the way in which they value experiences that, like the work, are destined to disappear.

Tibetan mandalas, for example, are created with great detail and dedication, only to be erased at the end of the process. This practice symbolizes the transitory nature of life and the need for detachment from material reality. This deliberate disappearance becomes an act of spiritual contemplation and a metaphor for the cycle of life, death and rebirth.

6.5.5. Temporality as a source of vitality

FINALLY, REFLECTION on temporality can be a source of vitality. When we recognize that time is limited, that each moment is unique and will never be repeated, a more intense appreciation of life is awakened in us. This awareness can lead to a fuller experience, to a greater appreciation of relationships, experiences and creations.

The carpe diem, or "seize the day", is a maxim that expresses this philosophy of life. It is an invitation to live urgently, to enjoy the present without procrastinating or leaving for tomorrow what can be experienced today. This attitude towards life, although motivated by the awareness of temporality, is not pessimistic, but fully affirmative: it embraces life in all its intensity because it knows that it is finite.

In this sense, the appreciation of temporality becomes a positive existential reflection, which motivates us to live with more awareness, to create with more passion, and to value every moment as a precious gift. Temporality is not just a limitation, but an opportunity to find a deeper and more authentic meaning in our existence.

6.5.6. Temporality as an existential reflection within the framework of artistic creation and aesthetic sensitivity.

WHEN WE TALK ABOUT "Temporality as an existential reflection" in the framework of artistic creation and aesthetic sensitivity, we are addressing how artists and creators not only recognize the ephemeral nature of life, but actively integrate it into their works as a central element. This integration of temporality into art opens a window to a deeper understanding of existence and transforms aesthetic sensibility into a tool for exploring and reflecting on the human condition, marked by transience and impermanence.

a. Transience as a theme and motif in art

TEMPORALITY, OR THE awareness of time as a force that erodes everything, has been a recurring theme in the history of art. Artists have often reflected the fragility of human life and the transience of experiences through motifs such as the passing of the seasons, the decay of material things, or the inevitability of death. This attention to transience is not only manifested in the content of the works, but also in the techniques and materials used.

The "vanitas" of Baroque painting, for example, are an artistic expression that embodies this reflection. These still lifes, full of symbols such as skulls, clocks, rotting flowers and luxury objects, not only represent temporality, but force the viewer to meditate on the inevitability of death and the insignificance of material possessions in the inexorable race of time.

Beyond iconography, transience also becomes a central motif in more contemporary art forms, such as instant photography or performance art, where the work of art exists only at the time of its creation or execution. Thus, the ephemeral is not only a theme of art, but an intrinsic quality of the work itself.

b. Art as a testimony to the ephemeral

ARTISTIC CREATION, especially in its most immediate and transitory forms, becomes a testimony to the ephemeral, not only as a theme, but also as a process. In performance art and temporary installations, the work of art dissipates at the very moment it is made, like a dance that leaves behind only the memory in the mind of the viewer.

A paradigmatic example of this sensitivity is the work of Marina Abramović, especially his performance *The Artist is Present* [95].

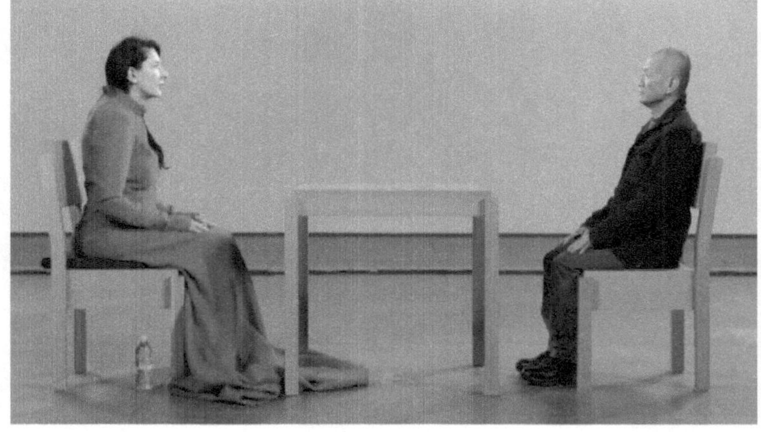

In this work, the central element is the ephemeral interaction between the artist and the viewers, a connection that develops in real time and disappears without a physical trace. Temporality here becomes the very medium of art, and the experience of the unique, unrepeatable moment becomes the key to a reflection on the transitory nature of life.

The ephemeral in art is also expressed in the use of temporary or degradable materials. British artist Andy Goldsworthy, for example, creates sculptures from natural elements such as stones, leaves or ice, which inevitably disintegrate over time[96]. This natural degradation is part of the work, making it a direct metaphor for the transience of all things:

[97]

c. Temporality in aesthetic sensibility

WITHIN THE FRAMEWORK of aesthetic sensitivity, temporality drives a way of perceiving and appreciating art that focuses on the present moment, on immediate experience. This sensitivity can be related to the concept of "aesthetic time," a form of time that is not measured by clocks or calendars, but by the intensity of the emotional and sensory experience that the artwork generates in the viewer.

This aesthetic time is manifested in a special way in the contemplation of works that are aware of their own transience. A clear example is the light installations by the artist Olafur Eliasson, where light and space combine to create an experience that is totally dependent on the immediate presence of the viewer[98]. These works are not permanent or fixed, but change and transform with the passage of time and the interaction of the public, reflecting the transience of the instant in which they are perceived.

[99]

THIS SENSITIVITY TOWARDS temporality can lead to a deeper form of aesthetic appreciation, in which the viewer is invited to be aware of the present moment and their own perception in that moment. Thus, ephemeral art and works that play with temporality not only represent the passage of time, but also transform the way in which the public experiences time.

d. Artistic creation as an existential reflection

TEMPORALITY ALSO DRIVES artistic creation as an act of existential reflection. Artists who work with the awareness of temporality often explore themes such as memory, loss, and constant change. These works can be seen as a way of facing one's own mortality, a way of giving shape and expression to the anxieties and hopes related to the passage of time.

A particularly interesting case is the work of Japanese filmmaker Yasujiro Ozu[100], whose films often focus on the small moments of everyday life, marked by the passage of time and changes in human relationships. His works, full of silence and contemplative pauses, remind us that life is a succession of ephemeral moments, each of which has a profound meaning precisely because of its fleeting nature.

In this sense, artistic creation becomes a way of dialoguing with temporality, of trying to understand and, perhaps, reconcile with the fact that everything is destined to disappear. This dialogue can take several forms: from the celebration of the moment to the exploration of memory as a form of preservation against oblivion. However, in all cases, art becomes a space where temporality becomes visible, where viewers are induced to contemplate and reflect on their own finite existence.

e. The beauty of the present moment and the joy of aesthetic pleasure

AESTHETIC PLEASURE can be understood as the deep satisfaction and appreciation we experience when witnessing or interacting with a work of art, a natural phenomenon or any manifestation that awakens our senses and emotions in a significant way. This pleasure is not limited to an immediate sensory response, but involves a deeper connection to the object or experience, often related to understanding, interpretation, and reflection.

The aesthetic joy of the instant refers to that pleasure experienced in specific and ephemeral moments, where the awareness of temporality intensifies the aesthetic experience. These moments can arise from unexpected situations or everyday circumstances that, under a certain light or perspective, acquire a special significance. For example, imagine a subway ride during rush hour. The crowd, noise, and constant movement can be overwhelming. However, at one point, a brief musical performance by a street performer fills the space with a melody that transforms the mood. Passengers, usually absent or distracted, let themselves be carried away by the music. This ephemeral moment creates an unexpected connection between strangers, generating an aesthetic pleasure that breaks the monotony of the journey.

Another example might be reading a poem in a public place, such as a library or a square. While we wait or simply walk, we find some verses inscribed on a wall or in a forgotten pamphlet. The power of words moves us and makes us reflect, generating a moment of unexpected aesthetic joy in the middle of the routine.

We can also consider the experience of contemplating a contemporary work of art that defies our expectations. In front of an installation that combines visual, sound and spatial elements in an innovative way, we find ourselves immersed in an alternative reality that invites us to reinterpret our perception. This moment of discovery and surprise gives us a deep aesthetic pleasure, the result of interaction with a singular artistic expression.

In the field of science, the observation of an unusual phenomenon can also generate aesthetic enjoyment. For example, researchers working with electron microscopy can discover shapes and structures at the molecular level that, in addition to their scientific interest, possess intrinsic beauty. The symmetry, patterns and textures observed can arouse an aesthetic admiration that enriches scientific experience.

One more case could be attendance at a spontaneous urban event, such as a collective artistic manifestation or a "flash mob"". The coordination and energy of the participants create an ephemeral show that transforms the public space and surprises casual spectators. This type of experience generates an aesthetic joy associated with surprise and temporary communion between participants and spectators.

These examples illustrate how the aesthetic pleasure of the moment is not limited to situations traditionally associated with beauty, but can emerge in everyday and even unusual contexts. The key lies in our ability to perceive and value these experiences, recognising the aesthetic richness that seemingly ordinary moments can offer. Philosophy of art and aesthetics have explored this phenomenon, highlighting the importance of a receptive and contemplative attitude towards the world. In this sense, Kant's aesthetic theory should be highlighted and its distinction between the concepts of bell and sublime. In the twentieth century, authors such as Walter Benjamin[101] have analysed how the aesthetic experience is transformed in the age of technical reproduction, while others, such as John Dewey[102], defend the idea that art and aesthetic experience are intrinsically linked to everyday life.

6.5.7 The Kantian sublime and the aesthetic joy of the instant

IMMANUEL KANT'S THEORY of art, particularly his notion of the sublime, offers an interesting perspective when examined in relation to the concept of the aesthetic joy of the instant. Kant defines the sublime as that experience that exceeds our capacity for understanding or representation, provoking a mixture of fear and admiration.

In his work "Critique of Judgment" (1790), Kant writes about the sublime:

"Sublime we call that which is absolutely great. [...] Sublime is that in comparison with which everything else is small."[103]

The Kantian sublime manifests itself when we are confronted with phenomena of such magnitude or power that they challenge our ability to fully grasp them. This can happen in the face of imposing landscapes, overwhelming natural phenomena, or even powerful abstract ideas. Kant illustrates it like this:

"The starry sky above me and the moral law within me. I see both things in front of me and immediately connect them with the awareness of my existence."[104]

In these moments, we experience a sense of overflow that, paradoxically, elevates us and makes us aware of our own rational capacity to conceive of the infinite or the absolute.

This experience of the sublime can be intimately related to the aesthetic joy of the moment. In both cases, there is an intensification of present consciousness, a momentary suspension of the ordinary temporal flow. The aesthetic joy of the instant involves a deep and immediate appreciation of the beauty or meaning of a specific moment, often accompanied by a sense of transcendence.

Kant describes this elevation of the mind by experiencing the sublime:

152

"The feeling of the sublime is, therefore, a feeling of pain that arises from the inadequacy of the imagination in the aesthetic estimation of magnitudes for estimation through reason; and it is, at the same time, a pleasure aroused by the fact that precisely this judgment of the inadequacy of the greatest sensible faculty agrees with the ideas of reason."[105]

The connection between the Kantian sublime and the aesthetic joy of the instant lies in its shared capacity for:

1. Break with the everyday perception of time and space.
2. Provoke an intensification of consciousness.
3. To generate a sense of transcendence or connection with something greater than oneself.
4. Producing a mixture of seemingly contradictory sensations (fear and pleasure, insignificance and grandeur).

Kant emphasizes this duality in the experience of the sublime:

"The mind is moved in the representation of the sublime in nature, while in the aesthetic judgment on the beautiful it remains in quiet contemplation. This movement can be compared (especially at its beginning) to a jolt, that is, to a rapid alternation of repulsion and attraction to the same object."[106]

In both cases, the aesthetic experience serves as a bridge between the finite and the infinite, between the tangible and the ineffable. Both the sublime and the joy of the moment allow us to experience, even if fleetingly, a connection with what is beyond our daily limitations.

This intersection between the Kantian sublime and the aesthetic joy of the instant highlights the ability of art and aesthetic experience to provide us with moments of deep meaning and spiritual elevation, reminding us of our inherent ability to transcend our perceived limitations and connect with larger dimensions of existence. As Kant concludes:

"Two things fill the mind with ever new and growing admiration and veneration, the more often and sustainably we take care to reflect on them: the starry sky above me and the moral law within me."[107]

7. INTERACTION BETWEEN ETHICS AND AESTHETICS IN THE PRESENT

The interaction between ethics and aesthetics in the present is an omnipresent phenomenon that permeates our daily experience. Imagine walking down a modern street: shop windows, advertising posters, even the architecture of buildings, all speak to us simultaneously in aesthetic and ethical languages.

Take, for example, the case of sustainable fashion. Stella McCartney, a pioneering designer in this field, has shown that ethics and aesthetics can not only coexist, but can reinforce each other. As she said, "I don't think you have to sacrifice style for the sake of being sustainable." This fusion of beauty and responsibility exemplifies what philosopher Yuriko Saito calls "the aesthetics of everyday life" in his book "Everyday Aesthetics" (2007)[108].

Yuriko Saito offers several concrete examples to illustrate the concept of aesthetics of everyday life. A particularly relevant example is that of lawn care in the American suburbs.

Saito explains how the aesthetic of a well-manicured and uniformly green lawn has become an ideal in many suburban neighborhoods in the United States. This aesthetic ideal, apparently harmless, has significant implications:

1. Environmental: Maintaining these lawns often requires the excessive use of water and chemicals, which can be harmful to the environment.

1. Social: The pressure to maintain a "perfect" lawn can create tensions between neighbors and influence community norms.
2. Economic: The cost of maintaining these lawns can be considerable for families.
3. Cultural: This aesthetic ideal reflects and reinforces certain cultural values about order and appearance.

Saito uses this example to demonstrate how a seemingly simple aesthetic preference in everyday life can have significant ethical, social, and environmental ramifications. He argues that being aware of these connections can help us make more informed and responsible decisions in our daily lives.

This example perfectly illustrates how the aesthetics of everyday life is intrinsically linked to broader ethical and practical issues, demonstrating the importance of critically considering our everyday aesthetic preferences.

In the field of contemporary art, artists such as Ai Weiwei have deliberately blurred the lines between aesthetic expression and ethical activism. His installation "Sunflower Seeds" (2010) at the Tate Modern[109] not only was it visually striking, but it also raised questions about mass production, individuality, and working conditions in China.

[110]

AS THE ART CRITIC ARTHUR Danto observed, contemporary art is no longer limited by traditional aesthetic considerations, and is free to explore a variety of projects and goals, which may include more conceptual or philosophical aspects.

"Contemporary art is too pluralistic in its intentions and realizations to allow itself to be captured in a single dimension. Beauty is an option for contemporary art, not a necessary condition. But with beauty as an option, it's as if art gets rid of itself and becomes free to pursue projects of all kinds." (The Abuse of Beauty, 2003)[111]

This interaction manifests itself in a particularly intense way in the digital age. Social networks such as Instagram have created a space where aesthetic decisions (what images we share) have immediate ethical implications (what values we promote). Media theorist Nicholas Mirzoeff, in his book "How to See the World" (2015), argues that in this context, "seeing is more than ever a matter of active participation".[112]

Architecture and urban design offer particularly tangible examples of this interaction. The architect Bjarke Ingels, known for projects such as the "8 House" in Copenhagen, defends a "pragmatic utopia" that seeks to harmonize aesthetic considerations with social and environmental needs. As he himself states:

"Architecture is the art and science of ensuring that our cities and buildings fit the way we want to live our lives."[113]

[114]

IN THE FIELD OF TECHNOLOGY, the aesthetics of digital interfaces have profound ethical implications. Don Norman, in his influential book "The Design of Everyday Things" (1988)[115], argues that good design is not only attractive, but also needs to be ethical and accessible. This idea has gained relevance in the age of mobile apps and social media, where interface design can influence user behavior in often subtle but meaningful ways.

Education plays a crucial role in navigating this intersection between ethics and aesthetics. Martha Nussbaum, in his book "Not for Profit" (2010)[116], argues that the humanities, including aesthetic appreciation, are essential for the formation of ethically responsible citizens. According to Nussbaum, "Education is not just for economic growth. It is above all for the nourishment of the democratic capacities of imagination and critical thinking".

In conclusion, the interaction between ethics and aesthetics in the present is not just a topic of academic debate, but a reality that influences our daily decisions, from what we buy to how we interact with our environment. Consciously acknowledging and navigating this interaction allows us, as the philosopher Alain de Botton suggests, to in "The Architecture of Happiness" (2006)[117], seek a "coherence between our internal values and our external environment". In doing so, perhaps we can aspire to a richer and more conscious life, where beauty and goodness inform and enrich each other.

7.1. How Immediate Aesthetic Judgments Influence Ethical Decisions

IN OUR EVERYDAY LIVES, immediate aesthetic reactions often subtly influence our ethical decisions, sometimes without us being aware of them.

Consider, for example, how the physical environment can affect our ethical behavior. A study conducted in a college cafeteria showed that students were more likely to clean their tables after eating when the space was decorated with fresh flowers and had pleasant lighting. In contrast, on days when the cafeteria was cluttered and poorly lit, students left the tables dirty more often. This example illustrates how an aesthetically pleasing environment can encourage more considerate and prosocial behaviors.[118]

The effect of aesthetics on ethical judgments is also manifested in how we perceive people. In a controversial experiment, a group of participants were asked to assess the guilt of a person accused of a crime based on a photograph. The results showed that the defendants considered more attractive were judged as less guilty, although the information about the case was identical. This "halo effect" demonstrates how aesthetic judgments can unfairly influence decisions with significant ethical implications.[119]

In the digital realm, the aesthetics of interfaces can subtly guide our ethical behavior. For example, a popular donation app found that changing the color of the "donate" button from gray to blue caused donations to increase by 10%. This illustrates how seemingly trivial design decisions can have a real impact on behaviors with ethical implications.[120]

Reactions of disgust, which have a strong aesthetic component, can also influence our moral judgments. One experiment showed that people were more likely to make harsh moral judgments when exposed to unpleasant odors or in a dirty environment.[121] This suggests that our immediate aesthetic perceptions may affect our assessment of complex ethical situations.[122]

Visual education and exposure to art can also influence our ethical sensitivity. A pilot program in primary schools that introduced regular visits to art museums observed an improvement in students' empathy and intercultural understanding.[123] This indicates that aesthetic education can be a powerful tool for moral development.

In this sense, the neuroscientist Semir Zeki, pioneer in the field of neuroaesthetics, suggests in his work that the same brain regions involved in aesthetic judgments are also involved in moral judgments. In an article published in "Trends in Cognitive Sciences" (2013), Zeki and colleagues write:

"There is considerable overlap between brain areas activated during moral and aesthetic judgments, suggesting a common neural basis for both types of judgments."[124]

Recognizing these influences is essential for more conscious and equitable decision-making. For example, many companies now use "blind" selection processes, where candidates' names and photos are removed to avoid biases based on immediate aesthetic judgments.

Ultimately, the intersection of aesthetics and ethics in our everyday experience underscores the importance of cultivating a more conscious and critical aesthetic sensibility. Not only does this enrich our appreciation of the world around us, but it also helps us navigate the complex ethical dilemmas we face daily in an increasingly visually and aesthetically stimulating environment.

7.2. The ethics of the aesthetic representation of the present

THE AESTHETIC REPRESENTATION of the present refers to the way we capture, interpret and present contemporary reality through various art forms and audiovisual media. This concept encompasses a wide range of creative practices that seek to reflect, comment on or interrogate the social, cultural, political and technological aspects of our current time.

This representation can manifest itself in multiple forms, including:

- Visual arts: painting, sculpture, photography, installations and digital art.

- Audiovisual media: cinema, television, video games, virtual and augmented reality.

- Media: photojournalism, documentaries, podcasts and online multimedia content.

- Design: graphic, industrial, architectural and user experience.

- Popular culture: fashion, music (both in its sound and visual form in music videos), and live performances.

- Public spaces: urban art, monuments, ephemeral interventions and interactive installations.

The inclusion of audiovisual media significantly expands the scope of the aesthetic representation of the present. For example:

- Film and television series not only offer visual representations, but use sound, dialogue and music to create a more complete and immersive representation of the present.

- Video games and virtual reality offer interactive experiences that allow users to "inhabit" and interact with representations of the present.

- Podcasts and other audio-based media contribute to the aesthetic representation of the present through soundscapes, oral narratives, and music.

The way in which the present is represented aesthetically raises important ethical questions about responsibility, authenticity, and power. In a world saturated with images and visual information, the way we choose to represent our current reality has significant implications for both our understanding of the world and the actions we take as a result.

One of the central debates in this field revolves around documentary photography and photojournalism. Susan Sontag, in his influential book "On Photography" (1977), raised crucial questions about the ethics of photographing human suffering. Sontag states:

"To take a photograph is to participate in the mortality, vulnerability and mutability of another person or thing. Precisely to cut a moment and freeze it, all the photographs testify to the ruthless dissolution of time."[125]

This observation raises questions about the responsibility of photographers and the media in the depiction of conflicts, disasters and other crisis situations. To what extent does the capture and dissemination of these images contribute to moral sensitization or, on the contrary, can it lead to a certain desensitization?

In the field of contemporary art, the artist Ai Weiwei He has directly addressed these ethical issues in his work. His installation "Law of the Journey" (2017)[126], which depicts a giant inflatable boat filled with anonymous human figures, is a powerful representation of the refugee crisis. Ai Weiwei has said about his work:

"Art has to be relevant to its time. It must question power and offer a voice to those who do not have one."

This statement underscores the ethical responsibility that many artists feel in depicting the cruel realities of the present.

[127]

THE QUESTION OF CULTURAL appropriation in contemporary art and design is another crucial aspect of the ethics of aesthetic representation, reflecting broader concerns about power, identity, and representation in contemporary society. In essence, it refers to the practice where artists from one dominant culture adopt or use distinctive elements from another, often minority or historically marginalized, culture in their work.

This phenomenon goes beyond simple artistic inspiration or influence. It involves complex questions about who has the right to represent or use certain cultural symbols, styles, or traditions. For example, when Picasso and other European Art Nouveau artists incorporated elements of African art into their works in the early twentieth century, opened a debate that is still present: is this type of adoption a form of homage and intercultural dialogue, or rather an exploitation of foreign cultural traditions?

James O. Young, [128] In her analysis of cultural appropriation in art, she suggests that this practice can be both problematic and potentially enriching. It can be problematic when it involves a lack of respect or a misrepresentation of the culture of origin, but it can also serve as a bridge for dialogue and cultural exchange. This duality is at the heart of many contemporary debates about appropriation in art.

Concern about cultural appropriation often arises from the imbalance of power between the cultures involved. When artists from a dominant culture take elements from a minority or historically oppressed culture, they run the risk of decontextualizing these elements, stripping them of their original or sacred meaning. In addition, when this adoption is commercialized, it can lead to situations where the dominant culture benefits economically at the expense of the source culture.

However, some argue that cultural exchange is inevitable and even desirable in an increasingly interconnected world. The artist Guillermo Gómez-Peña, for example, proposes to rethink appropriation as a cultural exchange, emphasizing the importance of genuine dialogue and mutual benefit:

"In our work, we try to erase the boundaries between 'us' and 'them', between art and life, between our multiple identities as artists, activists and citizens of the interconnected world."[129]

The debate on cultural appropriation in art also touches on fundamental questions about the nature of creativity and artistic freedom. Some artists argue that the ability to draw inspiration from and borrow elements from diverse cultures is essential for artistic innovation. Others, however, emphasize the importance of social responsibility and respect for cultural traditions.

Ultimately, the discussion of cultural appropriation in art reflects broader tensions in society about how we negotiate cultural differences in a globalized world. It forces us to consider how we can foster genuine and respectful cultural exchange, while acknowledging the histories of power and oppression that have shaped relations between cultures.

On the other hand, the use of technology in contemporary art raises new ethical questions. For example, the use of artificial intelligence in artistic creation sparks debates about authorship, authenticity and the value of human creativity. Art historian Joanna Zylinska, in his book "AI Art: Machine Visions and Warped Dreams" (2020), explores these questions and argues:

"AI-generated art is not simply a new form of artistic expression, but a mirror that reflects our own biases and assumptions about creativity and intelligence."[130]

Finally, the depiction of climate change and other environmental crises in art and visual media raises particular ethical dilemmas. How can we aesthetically represent phenomena that are often invisible or that develop on a time scale that goes beyond human perception? The artist Olafur Eliasson, known for its installations that address environmental issues, says:

"Art has the ability to change our perception of the world around us and, therefore, also our relationship with it. It can make what we normally take for granted visible and tangible." [131]

In conclusion, the ethics of the aesthetic representation of the present makes us consider not only what we represent, but how we do it and what are the consequences of these representations. In a world where images have immense power to shape perceptions and influence actions, the creation and dissemination of aesthetic representations of the present carries with it a great ethical responsibility. Artists, designers, and visual content creators face the challenge of navigating these ethical complexities as they seek to capture and communicate the realities of our time in meaningful and responsible ways.

7.3. Towards an integration of ethics and aesthetics in the experience of the present

LET'S IMAGINE A FUTURE where beauty and goodness are not separate concepts, but two sides of the same coin in our everyday experience. In this future, every decision we make, every object we create, and every space we inhabit reflects a deep integration between ethical and aesthetic considerations.

In our cities of the future, architecture and urban design not only seek to create visually appealing spaces, but also actively foster social interaction, sustainability, and psychological well-being. Buildings are not simply functional structures, but living works of art that breathe with the city, adapting to the changing needs of its inhabitants and minimizing their environmental impact. Public spaces become open-air art galleries, where interactive installations not only delight the senses but also educate and inspire ethical actions.

In the field of technology, we imagine digital interfaces that are not only intuitive and aesthetically pleasing, but are also designed to encourage healthy and ethical behaviors. The social networks of the future could use algorithms that not only display engaging content, but also promote diversity of perspectives and foster empathy. Video games could become powerful educational tools that combine captivating narratives with complex ethical dilemmas, helping players develop ethical decision-making skills while enjoying immersive aesthetic experiences.

In education, we can imagine a system that fully integrates the arts and humanities with science and technology. The schools of the future could be spaces where learning is a holistic experience that nurtures both aesthetic sensitivity and ethical reasoning. Students could learn mathematics through music, explore physics through dance, or study history through artistic creation, thus developing a deeper and more multifaceted understanding of the world.

In the world of work, the offices and factories of the future could be designed not only for efficiency, but also for the beauty and well-being of workers. We envision workspaces that incorporate natural elements, interactive art, and ergonomic designs that make work not only productive, but also an aesthetically pleasing and ethically satisfying experience.

In the field of consumption, we could see the emergence of a new ethics of product design where beauty, functionality and sustainability are inseparable. Everyday objects become small works of art that not only fulfill their function efficiently, but also constantly remind us of our responsibility towards the environment and society.

Public art could evolve into a form of social and environmental activism, creating aesthetic experiences that also inspire ethical actions. Imagine interactive murals that change in response to air quality, sculptures that collect rainwater to irrigate community gardens, or light installations powered by the energy generated by pedestrians.

In this future, political and social decision-making could also benefit from this integration. We imagine citizen participation processes that are not only effective, but also aesthetically appealing and emotionally satisfying, thus fostering greater civic engagement.

Ultimately, this integration of ethics and aesthetics into the experience of the present could lead to a more conscious and compassionate society. Living in a world where beauty and kindness are constantly intertwined, we could develop a keener sensitivity to both aesthetics and ethics in all aspects of our lives. This could result in a more harmonious society, where respect for the environment, social justice and personal fulfillment are not separate goals, but integral parts of the same vision of the good life.

8. FINAL CONCLUSIONS

Throughout this book we have explored the complex relationship between time, perception, ethics and aesthetics. We have examined how our understanding of the present influences our experience of the world, how immediate aesthetic judgments affect our ethical decisions, and how the representation of the present in art and culture reflects and shapes our reality. In this sense, we believe that the objectives we had set ourselves at the beginning of the work have been achieved, and that both the working hypotheses and the theses proposed have been confirmed from the observations and analyses that have been carried out.

Now, in conclusion, we propose an integrative vision that unites these threads in a coherent tapestry of what our future could be.

The integration of ethics and aesthetics in the experience of the present finds its deepest expression in the conscious experience of the moment. Imagine a future where the ability to fully perceive and appreciate the present moment becomes a fundamental skill, directly linking our aesthetic sensitivity with our ethical awareness.

In this future, the practice of mindfulness permeates every aspect of our existence. At every moment, we are fully aware of the beauty that surrounds us and the ethical implications of our actions. This heightened awareness of the present allows us to appreciate the ephemeral beauty of a stranger's smile or the harmony of an urban landscape, while making us more sensitive to the needs of others and the impact of our actions on the world.

Technology, education, work and art evolve to foster this awareness of the present. Schools cultivate the ability to live fully in the moment, companies value the quality of the present experience, and art creates experiences that intensify our perception of the now. Each area of life becomes fertile ground for the fusion of ethics and aesthetics.

This integration transforms our relationship with the environment, developing a deeper appreciation of the beauty of the natural world and a keener understanding of the urgency of protecting it. Every moment of contact with nature becomes a profound aesthetic experience and a reminder of our ethical responsibility to the planet.

Ultimately, this fusion of ethics and aesthetics in the experience of the moment leads us to a richer and more meaningful way of life. Every moment becomes an opportunity to experience beauty and to act with kindness. The distinction between what is beautiful and what is good is blurred, as we recognize that true beauty lies in actions and experiences that are both aesthetically satisfying and ethically correct.

Reflecting on the path we have traveled in this book, we see that this integrative vision is not just a distant dream, but a tangible possibility that we can begin to build right now. Each of us has the power to cultivate this awareness in our daily lives, to make decisions that harmonize ethics and aesthetics, and to live more fully in the present.

The implications of this perspective are profound, both individually and socially. As more people adopt this way of living, we could see a more conscious, compassionate, and creative society emerge. A society where beauty and goodness are not separate ideals, but integrated aspects of our daily experience.

However, how can each of us begin to incorporate this vision into our lives? What changes can we make today to live more fully in the present, to appreciate more deeply the beauty that surrounds us, and to act with greater ethical awareness? Is the future we have imagined an unattainable utopia, or a horizon towards which we can actively work? Perhaps the first step is to recognize and cultivate the connection between ethics and aesthetics in our everyday experiences, so that we can begin to build this more promising and optimistic future for the human species.

INDEX OF NAMES AND CONCEPTS

"

"But" (◈) 12

#Metoo 122

4

4'33 91

In

Action Painting 21
Low-Effort Activism 123
Adiaphorization 119
Ai Weiwei 149, 158
Alain De Botton 153
Albert Camus 133
Albert Einstein 27, 37, 52
Albert Heim 88
Alfred Mele 97
Non-standard analysis: 80

R

S

T

[1] Sylvie Droit-Volet (2011). "Child and Time". In Multidisciplinary Aspects of Time and Time Perception (pp. 151-173). Springer, Berlin, Heidelberg.

[2] "Ma is a Japanese word which can be roughly translated as 'gap', 'space', 'pause' or 'the space between two structural parts.' ... In Japanese, ma, the word for space, suggests interval. It is best described as a consciousness of place, not in the sense of an enclosed three-dimensional entity, but rather the simultaneous awareness of form and non-form deriving from an intensification of vision." Günter Nitschke. (1993). "Ma: Place, Space, Void". From Shinto to Ando: Studies in Architectural Anthropology in Japan (p. 49-61). London: Academy Editions.

[3] Whorf, B. L. (1956). Language, Thought, and Reality: Selected Writings of Benjamin Lee Whorf. MIT Press.

[4] In some Australian Aboriginal languages, such as that of the **Guugu Yimithirr**, absolute or cardinal terms such as "north", "south", "east" and "west" are preferred instead of egocentric terms, such as "right", "left", "front" or "back". This means that to refer to the location of an object or person, a speaker of these languages will not use referents related to their own position, but the position of the object with respect to an absolute frame of reference, linked to geographical directions.

There are cognitive implications that derive from this research. The work of Levinson and other researchers suggests that this constant use of cardinal directions profoundly influences the way speakers of these languages perceive and orient themselves in space. For example:

-Constant spatial orientation: Speakers of languages with a cardinal reference system have a much more developed sense of spatial orientation, as they need to be constantly aware of their relative position with respect to the cardinal directions. This can lead them to maintain accurate geographic orientation at all times, even when they are in enclosed spaces.

-Different spatial perception: Instead of conceiving space from an egocentric perspective (such as referring to "left" or "right" based on the position of one's own body), speakers of languages with absolute references see the world as a fixed structure. For example, instead of saying "the cup is on my right," they could say "the cup is on the northeast."

-Spatial memory and navigation: This way of speaking also affects spatial memory. People who use absolute reference systems tend to be more accurate in remembering the location of objects in relation to cardinal directions, which helps them navigate space more effectively, even in unfamiliar territory

See: Levinson, S. C. (2003). Space in Language and Cognition: Explorations in Cognitive Diversity. Cambridge University Press.

[5] "To see a World in a Grain of Sand, And a Heaven in a Wild Flower, Hold Infinity in the palm of your hand, And Eternity in an hour." (William Blake, "Auguries of Innocence" (1803))

[6] Einstein, Albert. Relativity: The Special and the General Theory. Methuen & Co., 1920.

[7] Heisenberg, Werner. Physics and Philosophy: The Revolution in Modern Science. Harper & Row, 1958.

[8] Rovelli, C. (2018). The Order of Time. Riverhead Books.

[9] Wesley C. Salmon, *Zeno's Paradoxes* (2001): "Zeno's arrow paradox, which argues that if time consists of discrete moments, then an arrow in flight is at rest at each instant. This reasoning challenges the very concept of motion if the universe is built from indivisible units of time" (*Salmon, 2001*, p. 13).

Salmon argues that the paradox is resolved by understanding that time and motion are continuously divisible. Movement cannot be conceived solely in terms of individual instants, since movement involves the transition between instants. The idea of time as a continuum is key: we cannot consider an object "immobile" in an instant if we analyze it in a context of change and motion:

"The resolution lies in rejecting the view that time consists of discrete, indivisible instants. Time and motion are continuous, and the passage between instants accounts for movement" (*Salmon, 2001*, p. 16).

[10] "Time is a moving image of eternity that moves according to number" (*Timaeus*, 37d)

"Plato defines time as the 'moving image of eternity'. This concept, found at 37d of the *Timaeus*, suggests that time, unlike eternity, is subject to change and measured through the celestial motions of the heavens, which Plato associates with the cosmos itself". Cornford, F. M. (1937): Plato's Cosmology. The Timaeus of Plato. London: Routledge & Kegan Paul. p. 115).

[11] "Time is the measure of movement according to the before and after." (Aristotle: *Physics*, Book IV, 11, 219b2).

[12] "What we now call the present, in fact, has no duration; it only exists because it is continually directed from the future to the past. If it were static, it would not be time but eternity." (St. Augustine: *Confessions*, Book XI, chapter 14)

[13] Augustine of Hippo: Confessions. Book XI, Chapter 15

[14] "Perhaps it would be more accurate to say that there are three times: a present of past things, a present of present things and a present of future things. These three kinds of time exist in a certain sense in the spirit, and I see them nowhere else: the present of the past is memory, the present of the present is vision, the present of the future is expectation." Augustine of Hippo. (2007). Confessions. Book XI, Chapter 20.

[15] "Eternity is the total, simultaneous and perfect possession of an endless life [...] God, who is always eternal, must be considered as always present. Its science, surpassing all temporal movement, remains in the simplicity of its presence and, embracing the infinite spaces of the past and the future, considers them in its simple knowledge as if they were fulfilled now." Boethius. (2002). The consolation of philosophy. Book V

[16] "Time is an accident that accompanies movement and is inherent to it. Neither exists without the other. Movement only exists in time, and the idea of time cannot be conceived if it is not with movement. Therefore, everything for which there is no movement does not enter under time." Maimonides, M: Guide to the Perplexed. Part II, Chapter 13

[17] Maimonides, M: Guide to the Perplexed I, 73, 106 a.

[18] Descartes, R. (1647). Metaphysical Meditations. Third Meditation.

[19] Malebranche, N. (1674-1675). Of the search for truth. Book VI, Part II, Chapter III.

[20] Kant, I. (1781/1787). Kritik der reinen Vernunft. A33/B49-50.

[21] G.W.F. Hegel: *Phenomenology of the Spirit* (*Phänomenologie des Geistes*) 1807, Chap: Sensible Certainty (Sinnliche Gewißheit), Volume 9, pages 91-95.

[22] Bergson, H. (1889). Essay on the Immediate Data of Consciousness. Chapter II: On the Multiplicity of States of Consciousness: The Idea of Duration.

[23] Heidegger, M. (1927). Sein und Zeit. § 68: Die Zeitlichkeit der Erschlossenheit überhaupt.

[24] Bohr, N. (1958). Atomic Physics and Human Knowledge. New York: Wiley. p. 20.

[25] Zadeh, L.A. (1973). Outline of a New Approach to the Analysis of Complex Systems and Decision Processes. IEEE Transactions on Systems, Man, and Cybernetics, SMC-3(1), 28-44.

[26] Bergson, H. (1911). Matter and Memory. London: George Allen and Unwin. p. 194.

[27] Priest, G. (2006). In Contradiction: A Study of the Transconsistent. Oxford: Oxford University Press. p. 1.

[28] In simpler terms, this formula is expressing a kind of "temporal consistency" for p. It's saying yes:

1. At any future point, if we find that p was true in the past, it will also be true at that future time, and

1. At any point in the past, if p was predicted to be true in the future, it was also true at that past moment,

1. Then p must be true now.

This formula is capturing the idea that p is a truth that remains consistent over time, both looking forward and backward. If p has this property of temporal consistency, then it must be true in the present.

It is a formal way of saying that if a proposition is "temporally robust" (it remains consistent when we look at it from any point in time), then it must be true in the present.

[29] Prior, A.N. (1970). "The Notion of the Present". Studium Generale, 23, 245-248.

[30] Deleuze, G. (1968). Difference and Repetition. Paris: Presses Universitaires de France.

[31] Deleuze, G. (1969). Logique du Sens. Paris: Les Éditions de Minuit

[32] Protention is the anticipation or projection into the immediate future that is an integral part of our experience of the present. While retention refers to the way in which the immediate past is held in present awareness, protension has to do with how the immediate future is anticipated in the present. Protension suggests that our consciousness is intentional, because it is always oriented towards the future, even in its experience of the present. For example, When we listen to a melody, we not only retain the notes we just heard, but we also anticipate the notes that will come, all as part of the present experience.

[33] Husserl, E. (1928): On the Phenomenology of the Consciousness of Internal Time.

[34] James, W. (1890): The Principles of Psychology, Vol. I. New York: Henry Holt and Company. Chapter IX: The Stream of Thought, p. 606.

[35] Merleau-Ponty, M. (1945). Phenomenology of perception. Paris: Gallimard. p. 477.

[36] Newton, I. (1687). Philosophiæ Naturalis Principia Mathematica. London: Joseph Streater. Scholium to the Definitions, p. 6.

[37] Collected in Dyson, F. (1979). "Time without end: Physics and biology in an open universe". Reviews of Modern Physics, 51(3), 447-460.

[38] Heisenberg, W. (1958). Physics and Philosophy: The Revolution in Modern Science. New York: Harper & Brothers. p. 58.

[39] Bergson, H. (1922). Duration and Simultaneity. Paris: Félix Alcan. p. 68.

[40] Varela, Francisco J., Thompson, Evan, & Rosch, Eleanor. The Embodied Mind: Cognitive Science and Human Experience. Cambridge, MA: MIT Press, 1991.

[41] See Prior, Arthur: Past, Present and Future (1967); Markosian, Ned: A Defense of Presentism, In Dean W. Zimmerman (ed.), Oxford Studies in Metaphysics Volume 1. Oxford University Press (2004)

[42] McTaggart, J.M.E. *The Unreality of Time.* Mind, Vol. 17, 1908.

[43] Carlo Rovelli – *Quantum Gravity* (Cambridge University Press, 2004).

[44] Lee Smolin – Three Roads to Quantum Gravity (Basic Books, 2001).

[45] Edward Witten – "Reflections on the Fate of Spacetime" a *Physics Today* (1996).

[46] Heisenberg, W. (1927). Über den anschaulichen Inhalt der quantentheoretischen Kinematik und Mechanik (On the Visual Content of Kinematics and Quantum Mechanics). Zeitschrift für Physik, 43(3–4), 172–198. doi:10.1007/BF01397280.

[47]

The Schrödinger equation is like a "guide" for predicting how particles behave at the quantum scale. Instead of describing exact trajectories (as is done with classical physics), the equation gives us the wave function, which tells us the probability of finding a particle at certain places and times.

For example, if we know the wave function of an electron in an atom, we can calculate what is the probability of finding that electron in a particular area around the nucleus. This probabilistic behavior is one of the key features of quantum mechanics, distinct from the determinism of classical physics.

Schrödinger, E. (1926). Quantisierung als Eigenwertproblem (Erste Mitteilung). Annalen der Physik, 79(361), 489–527. doi:10.1002/andp.19263840404.

[48]

The Copenhagen performance was mainly developed by Niels Bohr and Werner Heisenberg in the 1920s. This interpretation seeks to make sense of the probabilistic nature of quantum mechanics and the relationship between observation and quantum phenomena. He defends several key points:

- Wave function and probability: In quantum mechanics, the state of a system (such as an electron) is described by a wave function (Ψ), which contains all the information about the system. But this function does not tell us the exact position of the particle; It only gives us a probability of finding the particle in a certain position or with a certain value of other properties such as energy or momentum.

- The collapse of the wave function: According to this interpretation, when a measurement of a property of the system (such as the position of a particle) is made, the wave function collapses. Before the measurement, the wave function describes multiple possible outcomes (superposition), but once the measurement is made, only one of the possible outcomes becomes reality.

- Quantum indeterminism: In classical physics, you can accurately predict how an object will behave based on its current state. On the other hand, the Copenhagen interpretation tells us that at the quantum scale, the result of a measurement cannot be predicted with certainty; only probabilities can be given. This makes quantum mechanics fundamentally indeterministic.

- The role of the observer: Another important point of the Copenhagen interpretation is that the result of a measurement depends on the act of observing. That is, before the measurement, the properties of a particle (such as its position or momentum) are not determined, but exist in a superposition of possible states. The measure determines which of these possibilities becomes a reality.

- Schrödinger's cat metaphor: One of the best-known metaphors associated with this interpretation is Schrödinger's cat thought experiment. In this experiment, a cat is placed in a closed box with a quantum mechanism that can kill the cat or leave it alive. According to the Copenhagen interpretation, until the box is opened and a measurement is taken, the cat is in a state of overlap - both alive and dead at the same time. Only by opening the box and observing the result does the wave function collapse, and the cat is alive or dead.

See:

Bohr, N. (1935). *Can Quantum-Mechanical Description of Physical Reality Be Considered Complete?*tag. *Physical Review*, 48(8), 696–702. doi:10.1103/PhysRev.48.696.

Heisenberg, W. (1958). *Physics and Philosophy: The Revolution in Modern Science*. Harper & Row.

[49] Rovelli, C. (2004). *Quantum Gravity*. Cambridge University Press

[50] Rovelli, C. (2011). *The Order of Time*. Penguin Books. ISBN: 978-0241292525.

[51] Oriti, D. (2009). Approaches to Quantum Gravity: Toward a New Understanding of Space, Time and Matter. Cambridge University Press. ISBN: 978-0521860451.

[52] Hardy, L. (2007). Towards Quantum Gravity: A Framework for Probabilistic Theories with Non-Fixed Causal Structure. Journal of Physics A: Mathematical and Theoretical, 40(12), 3081-3099. doi:10.1088/1751-8113/40/12/S12

[53] see "Non-standard Analysis" by Abraham Robinson, 1966.

[54] see "Time and Modality" by Arthur N. Prior (1957)

[55] v. Approaches to Quantum Gravity: Toward a New Understanding of Space, Time and Matter" edited by Daniele Oriti (2009)

[56] see footnote 10

[57] "In God, all things are present in an eternal now. Therefore, the soul that merges with God enters into this now, where there is no past and no future." See: "Meister Eckhart: The Essential Sermons, Commentaries, Treatises, and Defense", translated and edited by Edmund Colledge and Bernard McGinn, Paulist Press, 1981.

[58] Salvador Dalí, "Dali by Dalí", 1970

[59] Chalmers, D. J. (1996). The Conscious Mind: In Search of a Fundamental Theory. Oxford University Press.

[60] Tononi, G. (2008). Consciousness as Integrated Information: a Provisional Manifesto. The Biological Bulletin, 215(3), 216-242. https://doi.org/10.2307/25470707

[61] Libet, B., Gleason, C. A., Wright, E. W., & Pearl, D. K. (1983). Time of Conscious Intention to Act in Relation to Onset of Cerebral Activity (Readiness-Potential). Brain, 106(3), 623-642. https://doi.org/10.1093/brain/106.3.623

[62] Dennett, D. C. (1991). *Consciousness Explained*. Little, Brown and Company.

[63] Eagleman, D. (2011). Incognito: The Secret Lives of the Brain. Pantheon Books.

[64] Blanke, O., Ortigue, S., Landis, T., & Seeck, M. (2002). *Stimulating illusory own-body perceptions. Nature*, 419(6904), 269-270. https://doi.org/10.1038/419269a

[65] Seth, A. (2014). A predictive processing theory of sensorimotor contingencies: Explaining the puzzle of perceptual presence and its absence in synesthesia. Cognitive Neuroscience, 5(2), 97-118. https://doi.org/10.1080/17588928.2013.877880

[66] Mele, A. R. (2014). Free: Why Science Hasn't Disproved Free Will. Oxford University Press.

[67] Gallagher, S. (2011). *The Overextended Mind*. In J. Reynard, M. L. Spock, & G. Thelen (Eds.), *Frontiers of Consciousness* (pp. 235-254). Oxford University Press.

[68] Tallis, R. (2011). Aping Mankind: Neuromania, Darwinitis and the Misrepresentation of Humanity. Acumen Publishing.

[69] See:

- Whorf, B. L. (1956). Language, Thought, and Reality: Selected Writings of Benjamin Lee Whorf. MIT Press.

- Sapir, E. (1929). *The Status of Linguistics as a Science. Language*, 5(4), 207-214.

[70] Nagarjuna. *The Fundamental Wisdom of the Middle Way* (trans. Jay L. Garfield). Oxford University Press, 1995.

[71] Thich Nhat Hanh Hanh. *The Heart of Understanding: Commentaries on the Prajnaparamita Heart Sutra.* Parallax Press, 1988.

[72] We could see a certain contradiction here. If there is nothing that has its own essence, how can we capture the essence of a tree in an eternal meditative instant? In Buddhism, the concept of "lack of one's own essence" (*sunyata*) means that no phenomenon exists autonomously, independent of other things. This implies that every phenomenon is empty of its own or fixed identity, because it is conditioned by a series of causes and conditions that are constantly changing. Thus, when a tree is said to have no inherent essence, it means that there is no permanent, fixed, or immutable nature that defines the tree independently.

On the other hand, when we talk about "capturing the essence" of a tree in a meditative moment, it is not a question of identifying a fixed essence of the tree, such as an immutable substance or an identity of its own. What is tried is to perceive the tree without the distortions imposed by the mind: without labelling, conceptualising or projecting previous ideas. It is more a matter of seeing the tree as it is in this moment, in a pure and direct way, in its present condition and interdependent with everything around it.

The idea of this direct perception is that, when you get rid of conceptualizations (such as labeling it as a "tree," defining its characteristics, or thinking of it as a separate entity), what remains is an experience that is not fragmented or mediated by duality. You are not capturing a "proper essence" of the tree, but its immediate reality, as it appears at that moment, without adding any notion of separation or permanence.

Thus, Buddhist practice does not seek to identify an essence that defines the tree in a static way, but to see the tree in its interconnection, as it manifests itself in that present moment, as one more part of the whole of reality. This meditative instant reveals the interdependent and empty nature of any phenomenon, freeing us from the illusion of fixed identities and the separation between subject and object. This leads us to the understanding that all phenomena share an interdependent and non-inherent nature, which is what we really perceive when we are conscious in this "eternal instant".

[73] THIS IS AN IDEA THAT connects directly with Kant's philosophy, when the philosopher from Königsberg argues that humans cannot directly access the "thing in itself" or "Noumen" (*das Ding an sich*), which is objective reality without our subjective interpretations or perceptions. According to Kant, we can only know phenomena as they appear to us through the filters of our mental categories (space, time, causality, etc.).

From this perspective, a direct experience of reality without distortions would be impossible because our entire experience is mediated by the way we perceive and conceptualize the world. That is, reality as it is (Buddhist "suchness") would always be out of our reach because our mind necessarily imposes structures on what we perceive.

Thus, while Buddhism aspires to transcend these distortions to achieve a "non-dual consciousness" and experience of reality as it is, Kant would argue that such an aspiration is metaphysically impossible. This discrepancy reflects two different views on the limits of human knowledge: a more transcendent and spiritual view in Buddhism and a more rational and limiting view in Kantian philosophy.

[74] Suzuki, Daisetz T. *The Lankavatara Sutra: A Mahayana Text*. Routledge, 2012.

[75] Conze, Edward. *Buddhist Thought in India: Three Phases of Buddhist Philosophy*. Ann Arbor Paperbacks, 1967.

[76] Dōgen (1999). *Shōbōgenzō: The precious vision of true dharma*. Translation by Dokushô Villalba. Barcelona: Ediciones La Liebre de Marzo.

Dōgen (1200–1253) was a Japanese Buddhist monk, philosopher, and founder of the Sōtō school of Zen in Japan. He is best known for his work **Shōbōgenzō**, a compilation of teachings that deeply explore the nature of reality, the practice of Zen, and the path to enlightenment. Dōgen traveled to China to study Chan Buddhism, and upon returning to Japan, he introduced the practice of **zazen** (sitting meditation) as a central method for spiritual realization.

[77] MUMON, WUMEN. *The Gateless Gate (Mumonkan)*. Trad. Koun Yamada. Wisdom Publications, 2004.

[78] Shapiro, S. L., Carlson, L. E., Astin, J. A., & Freedman, B. (2006). *Mechanisms of mindfulness. Journal of Clinical Psychology*, 62(3), 373-386. https://doi.org/10.1002/jclp.20237

[79] Carr, N. (2010). The Shallows: What the Internet Is Doing to Our Brains. W. W. Norton & Company.

[80] Greene, J. D., & Haidt, J. (2002). *How (and where) does moral judgment work?*tag. *Trends in Cognitive Sciences*, 6(12), 517-523. https://doi.org/10.1016/S1364-6613(02)02011-9

[81] Slovic, P. (2007). "If I look at the mass I will never act": Psychic numbing and genocide. Judgment and Decision Making, 2(2), 79-95.

[82] Fredrickson, B. L. (2001). The role of positive emotions in positive psychology: The broaden-and-build theory of positive emotions. American Psychologist, 56(3), 218-226. https://doi.org/10.1037/0003-066X.56.3.218

[83] Turkle, S. (2011). Alone Together: Why We Expect More from Technology and Less from Each Other. Basic Books.

[84] Ronson, J. (2015). So You've Been Publicly Shamed. Riverhead Books.

The case of Justine Sacco is a notorious example of the devastating consequences of social media. Justine Sacco, a public relations executive, was about to board an 11-hour flight from London to South Africa in December 2013. Just before boarding the plane, he posted a tweet that read:

"Going to Africa. Hope I don't get AIDS. Just kidding. I'm white!"

This comment, which was intended to be sarcastic or ironic, was considered by many to be insensitive and offensive, especially on the subject of racial inequality and the AIDS crisis in Africa. During the flight, she was offline, completely unaware of what was happening while she was sleeping or resting on the way.

Meanwhile, his tweet quickly went viral. Thousands of people reacted with outrage, sharing his comment and severely criticizing him on social media. The hashtag #HasJustineLandedYet became a phenomenon as people waited to see what would happen when Justine landed and realized what had happened during the flight.

When Sacco landed and turned on his phone, he discovered that he had become the top topic on Twitter globally, that his tweet had sparked a massive reaction of outrage, and that he had already lost his job at the PR firm where he worked. His reputation was shattered, and he was the subject of public humiliation on a global scale.

[85] Zuckerman, E. (2014). *New Media, New Civics? Policy & Internet*, 6(2), 151-168.

In this article, Ethan Zuckerman explores the phenomenon of "slacktivism", or low-effort activism, warning that the ease with which causes can be shared or supported online can give individuals a false sense of commitment and ethics, without leading to real change or meaningful commitment to the causes they are intended to support.

[86] Nissenbaum, H. (2010). *Privacy in context: Technology, policy, and the integrity of social life*. Stanford University Press.

[87] Floridi, L. (2014). *The fourth revolution: How the infosphere is reshaping human reality*. Oxford University Press.

[88] **Mono no aware** (◇◇◇◇[1]), literally "the pathos of things", and also translated as "an empathy towards things", or "a sensitivity to the ephemeral", is a Japanese[2] term for the awareness of impermanence (◇◇ *mujō*[3]), or the brevity of things, and both a soft transitory sadness (or melancholy) about his passing, as well as a longer and deeper sadness about the reality of life. https://es.wikipedia.org/wiki/Mono_no_aware

[89] Heidegger, M. (2009). *Being and Time* (J. E. Rivera, Trans.). Trotta. (Original work published in 1927).

[90] Sartre, J.-P. (2005). *Existentialism is a humanism*. Edhasa. (Original work published in 1946).

[91] Camus, A. (2014). *The Myth of Sisyphus* (L. Echávarri, Trans.). Alianza Editorial. (Original work published in 1942).

[92] Thich Nhat Hanh: The Heart of the Buddha's Teachings. Ed. Oniro, 1998

---

1. https://es.wikipedia.org/wiki/Ayuda:Idioma_japon%C3%A9s

2. https://es.wikipedia.org/wiki/Idioma_japon%C3%A9s

3. https://es.wikipedia.org/wiki/Ayuda:Idioma_japon%C3%A9s

[93] Fineberg, Jonathan. (2004). *Christo and Jeanne-Claude: On the Way to The Gates, Central Park, New York City.* New Haven: Yale University Press

[94] "The Gates," artists Christo and Jeanne-Claude's installation of 7,500 saffron-colored fabric panels hanging from 16-ft.-tall portals along 23 miles of walkway in Central Park, February 12, 2005, in New York City. CREDIT: TED THAI FOR TIME
Details

- Date: 2005-02-12
- Location: New York, NY, US
- Physical dimensions: COLOR TRANSMISSION
- Keywords of the subject: Christo-Javacheff, 2000s
- Publisher: TimeLife
- Usage: For personal non-commercial use only
- Provider: LIFE
- Copyright: © Time Inc.
- Credits: TIME
- Photographer: Ted Thai
- Original ID: TimeLife_image_13059027

[95] Biesenbach, Klaus (Ed.). (2010). *Marina Abramović: The Artist Is Present.* New York: The Museum of Modern Art.

[96] Goldsworthy, Andy. (1990). *A Collaboration with Nature.* London: Thames & Hudson.

[97]

- Title: Chestnut Circle
- Creator: Andy Goldsworthy
- Date of creation: 1989
- Origin: Acquired through the Henry Moore Foundation with support from the V&A Purchase Grant Fund, 1991

- Keywords of the subject: Natural Encounters
- Type: Natural Encounters
- Rights: © Andy Goldsworthy
- Technique: Chestnut leaves strung with chestnut twigs

Andy Goldsworthy: "At first I only used fallen leaves, relying on wind and frost to provide materials. I've been in the woods after a hard frost in the fall with noisy trees shedding leaves as the sun rose. There is a strangeness in the leaves that fall to the ground on a calm day, unlike the wind that can tear the leaves from the tree... The trees have taught me more. The biggest lesson is that many things can be found in something common and normal." [Goldsworthy, 1989] The chestnut tree circle is held together with small twigs of the chestnut tree, strung through chestnut leaves, which have then dried and contracted. No adhesive or glue has been used.

[98] GRYNSZTEJN, MADELEINE (Ed.). (2007). *Take Your Time: Olafur Eliasson*. San Francisco: San Francisco Museum of Modern Art.

[99] Exhibition dedicated to the artist Olafur Eliasson at the Guggenheim Museum Bilbao, 2020-2021

[100] Richie, Donald. (1977). *Ozu*. University of California Press

[101] Benjamin, W. (1936). *The work of art in the era of its technical reproducibility*

[102] Dewey, J. (1934). *Art as experience*. Perigee Books.

[103] Kant, I. (1790). *Critique of Judgment* (Critik der Urteilskraft) §25, Part II of Book I.

[104] Kant, I. (1790). *Critique of Practical Reason* (*Kritik der praktischen Vernunft*) Volume 5, page 161.

[105] Kant, I. (1790). *Critique of Judgment* (Critik der Urteilskraft) §27, part II of Book II.

[106] Kant, I. (1790). *Critique of Judgment* (Critik der Urteilskraft) §23, Part II of Book I.

[107] Kant, I. (1790). *Critique of Practical Reason* (*Kritik der praktischen Vernunft*) Volume 5, page 161

[108] Saito, Y. (2007). *Everyday aesthetics.* Oxford University Press.

[109] See: Black, Sandy. (2012). *The Sustainable Fashion Handbook.* London: Thames & Hudson.

[110]

Title: Sunflower Seeds
Creator: Ai Weiwei | Courtesy Ai Weiwei Studio
Date of creation: 2010
Rights: Courtesy Ai Weiwei Studio
Technique: Porcelain

[111] Danto, A. C. (2003). *The abuse of beauty: Aesthetics and the concept of art.* Open Court.

[112] Mirzoeff, N. (2015). *How to see the world: An introduction to images, from self-portraits to selfies, maps to movies, and more.* Basic Books.

[113] Ingels, B. (2009). *Yes is more: An archicomic on architectural evolution.* Evergreen.

[114] See: https://tecnne.com/arquitectura/8-house/

[115] Norman, D. A. (1988). *The design of everyday things.* Basic Books.

[116] Nussbaum, M. C. (2010). *Not for profit: Why democracy needs the humanities.* Princeton University Press.

[117] De Botton, A. (2006). *The architecture of happiness.* Pantheon Books.

[118] Keizer, K., Lindenberg, S., & Steg, L. (2008). The Spreading of Disorder. Science, 322(5908), 1681-1685.

[119] Robert Cialdini: "Influence: The Psychology of Persuasion" (1984)

[120] Paharia, N. (2013). Motivating consumers to donate: The impact of donation button design on charity websites. Journal of Consumer Psychology, 23(4), 498-511.

[121] Schnall, S., Haidt, J., Clore, G. L., & Jordan, A. H. (2008): "Disgust as Embodied Moral Judgment". Personality and Social Psychology Bulletin, 34(8), 1096–1109.

[122] Martha Nussbaum: "Hiding from Humanity: Disgust, Shame, and the Law" (2004)

[123] Greene, J. P., Kisida, B., & Bowen, D. H. (2014). The Educational Value of Field Trips. Education Next, 14(1), 78-86.

[124] Zeki, S., & Goodenough, O. (2013). *Law and the brain: Judgments, decisions, and the neural underpinnings of moral and aesthetic evaluations.* Trends in Cognitive Sciences, 17(9), 458-465. https://philpapers.org/rec/ZEKLAT

[125] Sontag, S. (1977). *On photography.* Farrar, Straus and Giroux.

[126] Ai, W. (2017). *Law of the Journey* [Art Installation]. National Gallery, Prague, Czech Republic.

[127] See: https://www.collater.al/en/the-law-of-the-journey-installation-ai-weiwei/

[128] James O. Young: "Cultural Appropriation and the Arts" (2010)

[129] Guillermo Gómez-Peña: "Ethno-Techno: Writings on Performance, Activism and Pedagogy" (2005)

[130] Zylinska, J. (2020). *AI Art: Machine visions and warped dreams.* Open Humanities Press

[131] Interview with Olafur Eliasson published in "The Art Newspaper", November 2018

Don't miss out!

Visit the website below and you can sign up to receive emails whenever Sergi Castillo Lapeira publishes a new book. There's no charge and no obligation.

https://books2read.com/r/B-A-ZDKDB-HKLCF

BOOKS2READ

Connecting independent readers to independent writers.

Also by Sergi Castillo Lapeira

Biblioteca de la Natura
Gully, the Shark That Wanted to Know Himself

Standalone
La vida de George. Historia de un humano sintético
Diálogos filosóficos con mi amigo Pi
Philosophical dialogues with my friend Pi
Inspector Montoliu
Inspector Montoliu. The Case of the Unknown Twin
Una Historia Sentimental
The Life of George. Story of a Synthetic Human
Cuentos a la orilla del hielo
Gina, la jirafa que quería ser libre
Gina, the Giraffe Who Wanted to Be Free
Gully, el tauró que es volia conèixer a si mateix
Ethics and Aesthetics of the Instant in the Digital Age
Ética i Estética del Instante en la Era Digital
Ètica i Estètica de l'Instant en l'Era Digital

Watch for more at https://edicionsmataro.com/.

About the Author

En Sergi Castillo Lapeira va néixer a la ciutat de Mataró l'any 1959. Va estudiar a la Universitat de Barcelona, on es va llicenciar en Filosofia i Ciències de l'Educació el 1984, i en Filologia Catalana el 1996.

Del 1984 al 2022 va treballar com a professor de filosofia a l'Escola Pia Mataró, on també va participar en la posada en marxa de la Reforma Educativa.

Ha publicat tres novel·les, un llibre de poesia, un llibre d'assaig i un recull de contes, tots ells disponibles a:

edicionsmataro.com

Read more at https://edicionsmataro.com/.